PENGUIN BOOKS

The Hidden Canyon

Home for John Blaustein is Berkeley, California—that is, when photographic assignments do not find him elsewhere. Elsewhere might be Europe, where during the summer of 1977 he went in search of houseboats, or South America, where in 1976 he combined his dual skill as photographer and boatman to river-journey through the jungles of Surinam. The photographic results of both trips will illustrate future books. His color photography, which has been exhibited at The San Francisco Art Institute, has appeared in *Smithsonian* and *Popular Photography* magazines, as well as in Time Life Books' "American Wilderness" and "Boating" series and in *The Plant Book: The Complete Guide to Healthy House Plants* by Bill Henkin and Maria Vermiglio. John Blaustein has served as guide and boatman on more than thirty-five dory trips down the Colorado River. Would he do it again? "Absolutely."

Occasional park ranger, fire lookout, and lecturer, and full-time wilderness poet and environmentalist, Edward Abbey adopted the Southwest as his homeland in 1947, following a cross-country trip that took him through this canyon, desert, mountain, and forest land. He has since also adapted the rich Southwest landscape as the backdrop to many of his novels and short stories. Mr. Abbey is the author of *Desert Solitaire*, *Slick Rock*, *The Brave Cowboy* (the basis for the film *Lonely Are the Brave*), *Fire on the Mountain*, *Cactus Country*, *Appalachia*, *Black Sun*, and *The Monkey Wrench Gang*. His ambition is to write "a monstrous tome—or tomb—of exactly 1000 fine-print pages." It would also make him infinitely happy to witness the annihilation of the Glen Canyon Dam.

Former director of the Sierra Club, Martin Litton is president of Grand Canyon Dories, Inc., the outfit that has taken more than two thousand people through the Canyon by small wooden dory since it began public operation in 1969. It is the only group that sponsors the trip in motorless rigid craft. Mr. Litton lectures extensively on the preservation of America's wild and scenic rivers; he is passionately opposed to the construction of dams—and other obstacles—that impede the remaining free-flowing waters of the world.

The Hidden

John Blaustein

Canyon A River Journey

A Journal Edward Abbey   *Introduction* Martin Litton

PENGUIN BOOKS

To my parents,
who gave me the freedom
to choose photography and river boating,
and to Martin and Esther Litton,
who gave me the Grand Canyon.

—J.B.

Penguin Books Ltd, Harmondsworth, Middlesex, England
Penguin Books, 625 Madison Avenue, New York, New York 10022, U.S.A.
Penguin Books Australia Ltd, Ringwood, Victoria, Australia
Penguin Books Canada Limited, 2801 John Street, Markham, Ontario, Canada L3R 1B4
Penguin Books (N.Z.) Ltd, 182–190 Wairau Road, Auckland 10, New Zealand

First published in the United States of America in simultaneous hardcover and
paperback editions by The Viking Press and Penguin Books 1977

Library of Congress Cataloging in Publication Data
Blaustein, John, 1947–
The hidden canyon.
1.   Boats and boating—Colorado River.   2.   Colorado
River—Description and travel.   I.   Abbey, Edward,
1927–   II.   Title.
[GV776.C63B55   1977b]   917.88′1   77–9546
ISBN 0 14 00.4678 X

Printed in Japan by Dai Nippon Printing Co., Ltd., Tokyo
Set in Linotype Janson

Contents

Preface

Previous to my initial meeting with Martin Litton in 1970, I had seen the Grand Canyon only twice from the rim, and had hardly noticed the river way down at the bottom. I certainly didn't know that it is the roughest stretch of navigable water in North America. As I had never seen a dory or a rapid, and knew little about camping, it was with limited enthusiasm that I agreed to serve as the cook's assistant during the first of the two dory trips Martin was planning for that summer. Three weeks before the first trip was to begin, Martin phoned and asked if I would be available for both trips, explaining that he needed an extra boatman on the second. Though he knew I had never held an oar, he assured me that rowing a dory down the Colorado was simply a matter of keeping the bow turned straight into the waves and following the dory just in front of mine through the rapids. There would be plenty of time for me to learn to handle a boat during quiet stretches in the first trip.

I wasn't much help to the cook on that first trip, but I did learn which oar to pull in order to pivot the boat. By the end of the trip I was reasonably confident that I could get from Lee's Ferry to Lake Mead in one piece if I managed to stay close behind one of the experienced boatmen.

Following another boat turned out to be a bit

more difficult than I had expected. Somehow, no matter how closely I pursued, the first boat would inevitably vanish over the edge as it dropped into the tongue at the head of a rapid. By the time my boat was close enough for me to see, it was too late to tell exactly what the first boat had done. I'd find myself completely lost at the top of the rapid, beyond the point of no return. All I could see was churning whitewater, huge waves and holes everywhere, with no clear route through. At times it was downright terrifying. All I could do was attempt to hit the waves as straight as possible, and hope I wouldn't collide with any rocks.

The first two days were fine, but on the third I flipped in 23 Mile Rapid. Then, on the sixth day, I hit a rock in Unkar Rapid that almost broke the boat in half. Martin admitted that the dories had been banged up before, but never that much at one time! Since all the materials needed to fix a damaged boat are brought along, we were able to patch up my dory without too much trouble.

With all my attention on learning to row, I didn't take very many pictures that first summer. Those that I did take were in black and white, and not very encouraging. I knew I wanted to go back—two trips were enough to get me hooked on rowing the rapids in a dory. I also wanted to photograph some more, and thought I would use color film the next time. It would be my first experience with color.

There were four trips in 1971. Though my previous year's performance as a boatman left much to be desired, Martin generously agreed to give me another chance. Much to everyone's relief, including my own, my rowing technique did improve and I made it through the summer without hitting any more rocks. I did tip over three times, but in those days tipping was fairly common and created no major problem. (I still can't understand why many of our passengers actually relish the thought of being in a boat that goes over. I've always felt the rapids were sufficiently exciting without having to bob up and down in the water in a life jacket.) Today, the boatmen are so experienced that most trips get through the Canyon with no flips at all.

I have gone back to the Canyon every summer since 1971, for the dual purpose of rowing and photographing. The pictures in this book are a record of over thirty eighteen-day trips. Regardless of where photo assignments may lead me in the future, I'll continue to return to the Canyon: it's impossible to get the river bug out of one's system once it establishes a firm grip!

John Blaustein

Introduction

This book is not a place for Grand Canyon statistics. The things expressed in John Blaustein's photographs and Edward Abbey's words are not derived from charts and numbers but from the majesty and fragility of the place, and from the human response to it. It would have been wasteful of space and energy for either Ed or John to go into a lot of detail that is already at hand; for the best of that, complete enough for any inquisitive mind and set down with polish and charm, I suggest Francois Leydet's original folio-scale *Time and the River Flowing: Grand Canyon.*

However, there are *facts* about the Grand Canyon of the Colorado River that ought to be straightened out right here.

To begin with, the Canyon is entirely in northwestern Arizona. The river that flows through it is mostly the result of the union, in eastern Utah, of the Green River from Wyoming and the Colorado River. Long established as the Grand River, it was legislated otherwise in 1921 by Congress at the insistence of Colorado, the state of its Rocky Mountain origins.

The length of the Grand Canyon, along the river's course, was measured by the United States Geological Survey in 1923. The Canyon begins at Mile Zero and ends at Mile 277, and quite plainly has a length of 277 miles, not 217, a figure well suited to the intrigues of the Bureau of Reclamation* but also adopted by dictionaries, by authors who ought to know better, and—in an incredible affront to the intelligence of some two million Grand Canyon visitors per year—by the National Park Service in a bold, dogmatic exhibit at Mather Point, far and away the most-visited overlook on either rim.

Now, what could be behind all that? Several things, as we shall see. Mile Zero, where the Navajo sandstone of Glen Canyon ends and the Kaibab limestone of the Grand Canyon first appears at the surface, is just downstream from the site of the ferry established and operated (1872–74) by the Mormon leader John Doyle Lee, then a fugitive for having commanded the massacre of 123 westbound emigrants at Mountain Meadows in southwest Utah in 1857. Below Lee's Ferry the Canyon, trending southwestward with the river, deepens at the rate of about one hundred feet to the mile for a good twenty-five miles into the gradual rise of the East Kaibab

* The Bureau of Reclamation, originally established in order to reclaim land in the West for agricultural purposes, eventually became involved in flood control, irrigation, hydroelectric power, and so on.

Monocline. The monocline is an upward bend of strata, forming the east side of the broad uplift of land that the river, cutting crookedly somewhat south of center, has divided into two plateaus—the larger, higher Kaibab to the north and the Coconino to the south.

There is nothing gradual about the lower end of the Canyon. When you are on the river, hemmed in by soaring cliffs for 277 miles and, perhaps, for a period of two to three weeks, it's something of a shock to round a bend into open sky and find that you are out. Along the north-south escarpment of the Grand Wash Cliffs, the elevated country that began with that gentle slant of the earth's crust at Lee's Ferry, walling in your personal cosmos, ends only too abruptly.

Hardly anyone questions the evidence that the river—helped, naturally, by weathering and erosion of the rocks along its sides—dug the Canyon, but there are a couple of conflicting ideas as to how this was done. Did the river maintain an established meandering course through land that was slowly rising (the long-held assumption based on the river's meandering entrenchment, independent of geological structure, in the plateau), or did it begin as two rivers, the upper one blocked off by the *already* uplifted plateau and the lower (western) one eventually cutting back through the plateau to "capture" it?

This latter theory further assumes that, before the capture, the upper river curved southward, away from the Colorado's present course, at a point sixty miles downstream from today's Mile Zero, and flowed off into a dead-end lake. When headward erosion by the western stream finished cutting through the plateau, the combined flows then ran west through the plateau, deepening the main canyon so that the lake drained back into it, reversing the gradient of the upper river's former channel to the lake, and thus creating the gorge now occupied by the inflowing Little Colorado River. Take your pick of the theories; what I am getting at is that the Little Colorado, running north to enter the main stream at Mile 60, comes down a big, spectacular side canyon, often dry in its upper reaches, which affords reasonably hazard-free access and egress for anyone not deterred by the prospect of a long hike. Therein lies the basis for misconception as to the size of the Grand Canyon.

The origin of the name Grand Canyon is obscure. But think of this place, discovered by Europeans in 1540, known to the world and looked into from its rims for 329 years before anyone saw all of the bottom of it from the level of the river!

That was first done in 1869 by a party of ten men led by a one-armed Civil War veteran, Major John Wesley Powell. Rowing and dragging narrow round-bottomed boats, they went from the town of Green River, Wyoming, to the Colorado's confluence with the Virgin River, in southern Nevada, in a little over three months.

In some quarters there is still belief in the claim of James White (not the Jim White who discovered Carlsbad Caverns) that in 1867, to escape pursuit by Indians in Glen Canyon, he jumped on a mass of floating debris and drifted all the way through the Grand Canyon in a couple of weeks without food or rest. Anyone who knows the Colorado River's ways in the Grand Canyon knows that that could not have happened. Powell's men, river-wise by the time they entered the Grand Canyon near the end of their ordeal, and working desperately against time every inch of the way, took a good deal longer than that. Without propulsion, most floating objects soon drift against or onto the banks before they get very far into the Canyon, and those that do float all the way through take a long time, sometimes years. The body of Peter Hansbrough, who drowned in the upper reaches of the Canyon during a survey trip in 1889, had floated only eighteen miles downstream when it was found, six months later, circling slowly in an eddy at Mile 43. It matters not that the average speed of the water in the river is about three and one-half miles per hour; powerful countercurrents and calm bays tend to trap and hold anything that floats. At some volumes of flow, there are stretches where the entire surface of the river, from bank to bank, moves constantly upstream.

White did come out of the lower end of the Canyon in 1867, badly exposed, sunburned, starving, and incoherent, but just where he got onto the river will always remain a mystery. He may not have meant to perpetrate a hoax: remember, there were no maps in those days—there would not even be a state of Arizona for another forty-five years—and there really was no way for him to know where he was.

So Powell was the first. His voyage, however, did not signal a rush of traffic down the Grand Canyon; few men wanted to go off and chance death for no good reason, and Powell's reports were not exactly calculated to allay apprehensions. But in time the possessing tug of wilderness would be felt by more and more, and by the year 1950 the total number of persons who had floated the river was one hundred. Historian Dock Marston, the man who knows, tells us that my wife and I were Nos. 185 and 186 (the order depending, of course, on who was at which end of the boat at the finish); that was in 1955, so the snowball was beginning to roll. In 1977 alone, the count will reach about fourteen thousand, but the annual number has actually diminished since 1972, when limits were first put into effect by the National Park Service. With no more than fourteen thousand people spread over a distance of some two hundred miles throughout a river-running season that lasts four or five months, only the most reclusive among us will feel that the glorious river trail through the Grand Canyon—easily the longest, wildest, grandest whitewater route in the world—is overcrowded.

Sixty miles into the Grand Canyon, Powell reached the mouth of the Little Colorado. Rations were short; much equipment had been lost to the tumultuous waters far upstream; exhaustion seemed imminent. He knew, from the Hopi Indian practice of coming down this tributary canyon on ceremonial occasions to mine salt near the confluence, that here was a way out, in all probability the last chance to escape the unknown dangers that lay ahead. Writing in his "journal" years later (he did not do much writing during the trip), he recalled the bleak prospects in what has become his most-quoted passage: "We are ready to start on our way down the Great Unknown. We have an unknown river yet to run, an unknown canyon to explore. . . ." From this graceful turn of phrase, and from nothing else, was derived the quaint notion that the Grand Canyon ought to be thought of as beginning at the Little Colorado.

The Bureau of Reclamation picked up or cooked up the term "Marble Canyon" for the upstream reach; after all, there would be much easier sledding for a dam at Mile 39 if people did not regard it as a desecration of the *Grand* Canyon.

There is no marble along the Colorado River. What Powell romantically referred to as marble—the Redwall limestone, six hundred feet thick and at 355 million years still rather youthful as Grand Canyon rocks go—first appears at Mile 23 and forms continuous bands of rosy-stained vertical cliffs at somewhat varying elevations on both sides of the river all the way to the end of the Canyon. There is nothing in the Grand Canyon to warrant a differentiation between its first sixty miles and the rest of it.

The distance from the Little Colorado to the Grand Wash Cliffs is 217 miles. In an exasperating perpetuation of foolishness, government and encyclopedias cling to that figure as the length of the Grand Canyon. But that glassed-in affair at Mather Point outdoes everything else, as it boldly proclaims 217 Miles as the measured distance *from Mile Zero at Lee's Ferry to the old Pierce Ferry landing at Mile 280*. The Grand Canyon does not need overstating or stretching, of course. But some people need to place a little more faith in Major Powell's brainchild, the Geological Survey.

·   ·   ·

In the long-term perspective of a canyon millions upon millions of years old, carved inch by inch down into a rising plain of which the youngest rocks—the upper Permian surface formation we call the Kaibab—are a couple of hundred million years old and the oldest—the mysterious flinty schists of the innermost gorges—still glitter with the dawn-light of Creation, it seems almost funny to worry about what we do to it. The proud dams above and below, those ugly concrete plugs Ed Abbey would like to blow up, are at worst fleeting aberrations. And though there is much concern over what we may be instigating in the Canyon by traveling through it on rafts and in boats, there seems to be widespread agreement that we are scarcely leaving enough twentieth-century artifacts and drowned corpses behind to provide a decent fossil record of our times in the siltstone forming under Lake Mead.

If for nothing more than the enjoyment, instruction, and inspiration of the transitory race called human, we should be determined to sustain the river experience in the Grand Canyon. Few things in this world are really beyond description, but it is safe to say that the exhilaration attendant upon entering and running a big Grand Canyon rapid in a small boat is one of them. Add to the scores of rapids the compelling subjects for contemplation (including, at times, the responses of your fellow wayfarers, and yes, even the sandstorms, rainstorms, and the inevitable cuts and bruises) and there is nothing more, with the possible exception of a hot shower now and again, that anyone should ask of life.

The rules and regulations governing activities along the canyon rims and down the trails have more than kept pace with the growth of traffic on the river. If you view them as incontrovertible law, it is now illegal to do quite a few things traditionally done on wilderness outings by normal folks. Aside from the prohibition against doffing your life jacket even if the nearest riffle is five miles away, the ordinances are in recognition of the worsening (from the human point of view) scarcity of camping space along the river as the daily surge from the power plant of Glen Canyon Dam scoops away at what is left of the beaches. Someone else will come along, looking for a good place to bed down, within a few days after you vacate your camp. So you don't build a fire that will leave soot on the ground, or throw out the dishwater, or go to the toilet where there is no toilet, unless you are a long way from the river. These constraints are matters of courtesy as well as regulation, so that there will be as little evidence as possible of your passage to offend later visitors. But also, out of respect for the more or less defenseless forms of native life, you don't walk in small streams or shampoo your hair in them, and you step aside for bumblebees, tarantulas, and snakes.

· · ·

The first time I saw Edward Abbey he was not yet famous, so it must have been eight or nine years ago. Our party was at Lee's Ferry, readying our beautiful Grand Canyon Dories for a three-week trip. In those gentler, less pressured times we had not yet been ordered down to the hot gravel flat where the big motorized baloney boats were inflated and rigged for launching. Our mooring lines ran up through the horsetail and grasses into the shade of an old willow tree where Abbey, having mentioned that the reason he was wearing a National Park Service shirt was that he was a combination truck driver and substitute ranger there to inspect our put-in, sat drinking a can of our beer. It was not until I saw his picture on the jacket of *Desert Solitaire*, long enough afterward for him to have grown a beard and to have gotten into print, that I remembered the name on the nameplate under the big easy grin back there on the riverbank.

After *Desert Solitaire*, the embarrassed Interior Department (they embarrass readily, as well they should) tried to keep Abbey out of sight. No fire-lookout tower was too remote to be his assigned station; I imagine that before he parted company with the Park Service he had many a quiet hour with little to do but put rebellious publishable things on paper at government expense.

He loves to shock, and does it well in writing, although he just can't bring it off in person. With letdown or relief, or more often both, we one day run up against this iconoclast, this rebel with cause, this terrorist of the typewriter, this Bolshevik with lighted fuses sputtering from every pocket and even from his inside-out cowboy boots, and we find him the gentlest of men, seeming unsure of himself in human company, and always the soul of conservatism.

Edward Abbey is hardly alone in his protest. In their way, the dories are elements of *our* protest, but by no means all of it. For the next eighteen days, three of the seven dories—the *Tapestry Wall*, the *Moqui Steps*, and the *Music Temple*—will keep reminding Abbey of the hateful dam that motivated *The Monkey Wrench Gang* after burying these wonders of Glen Canyon under the water of "Lake" Powell.

•   •   •

Incredibly, everything is stowed—all the things we need plus the things the government says we need. Author Abbey, unaccustomed to being guided and cared for by others, looks a bit self-conscious as he perches, in a bright new life vest, beside his lovely bride Renée in the *Peace River*, but he will get over that as the canyon days unfold. This is a scheduled public trip in which the twenty-two participants ("passengers" does not seem quite right, somehow) are of ages twelve through seventy-seven, from all walks of life, as they say, and from all over the country and one or two foreign countries to boot. For the next seventeen nights they will sleep on the ground, and in the days between they will drift through gorges no artist could ever depict and crash through cataracts no open-water sailor would ever believe. When they feel like it, they will explore ashore, up the side canyons to secret springs and gardens and to the ancient buildings where vanished races dwelt a thousand years ago. They will watch the bighorn's leaping ascent of the cliffs, the eagle's soaring flight along the rimrock. They will get to know the beavers, ravens, ouzels, wood rats, lizards, and cacomistles that have never learned to fear humans because they have never had to. They will see the horrors wrought upon the Canyon by the Bureau of Reclamation's test diggings at Mile 39 ("Marble damsite") and by the National Park Service's channelization of Bright Angel Creek into a riprapped storm drain at Mile 88. And occasionally they will meet other parties, most of them traveling by baloney boat.

One of our oarsmen-guides is John Blaustein. Years have been speeding by, and it's hard to keep in mind that John was only twenty-two when he wangled his way into our outfit as cook's helper. When he did get a boat on his second trip, I had to keep admonishing him to stop telling the passengers how frightened he was every time he approached a rapid. A shade too clean looking to fit the image of a river guide, he was a bit slow in gaining acceptance, but when it did come it was complete, and he now ranks at the top, not only for handling a spirited dory in whitewater but also as a host and guide.

I don't know when John Blaustein decided to become a photographer, but his artistry with a camera does not need to be proved by listing his honors here. All you have to do is turn the page.

Martin Litton

A Journal EDWARD ABBEY

DAY **1** Bright-eyed and bushy-tailed, we assemble at Lee's Ferry, Arizona, on the banks of the brand-new cold green Colorado River. Green because of microplankton. Cold because this water is issuing from the bottom of a dam twelve miles upstream—that Glen Canyon Dam. The temperature of the water here is 47° F. (I place a six-pack of Michelob in the water for quick chilling.) And brand new? This river is not the Colorado we knew and loved. The real Colorado died in 1964 when the engineers of the Bureau of Reclamation closed the gates at Glen Canyon Dam, changing the Colorado from a wild and free river into the domesticated, well-regulated conveyor belt for baloney boats that it is today. Probably no man-made artifact in all of human history has been hated so much, by so many, for so long as Glen Canyon Dam.

There's John Blaustein himself, loading his little wooden boat, a dory called *Peace River*. He looks anxious. Can't blame him. He has many problems on his mind—cameras, the passengers, the rapids.

His boss, one Martin Litton, who owns and manages Grand Canyon Dories, is hanging around nearby. Nine years ago I was the ranger here at Lee's Ferry. I used to squeeze Martin's life jackets, testing them for safety.

"Look here, Martin," I say, giving one of his flimsy boats a kick in the slats, "you don't really expect us to float down the river and run the rapids in a thing like this. What's it made of, plywood? One rap on a rock and it'll crack like an egg." Talking of old times and new problems, he ignores my facetious fears.

I turn my attention to the boatmen and to my fellow passengers on this suicidal journey down the river of no return.

There are seven dories, bright and gaily painted craft, each named after some natural feature destroyed or maimed by the works of man: the *Peace River* (dammed in Canada); *Tapestry Wall*, *Moqui Steps*, *Music Temple* (lovely places in Glen Canyon now sunk beneath the stagnant waters of Lake Powell National Sewage Lagoon); the *Vale of Rhondda* (a ravaged coalfield in Wales); and the *Columbia* and the *Celilo Falls* (drowned by the Dalles Dam on the Columbia River). The boats are about seventeen feet long from stem to transom, seven feet wide at the beam. Closed hatches at bow, midships, and stern make them virtually unsinkable, we are told.

An obvious lie. I don't believe it for a moment. "Virtually unsinkable." "Virtually" indeed. What sinister ambiguities are contained in that sly equivocation? Why not say "virtually floatable?" How about "virtually sunk," "virtually drowned," or "virtually dead?" Yeah, *virtually*; I can see through this transparent scheme. It's a conspiracy to get us down there among those awful wavelets in the Paria Riffle. Asphyxiation.

And the boatmen, they look even worse than the boats. Seven little wooden boats and seven furtive, grinning boatmen with fourteen hairy, crooked legs. They look like overgrown gnomes. I feel like Snow White, stumbling into the wrong fairy tale. A Disneyfied nightmare. Time to back out of this deal. I knew there was something queer about the whole setup, this supposedly free ride on the new Grand Canyon subway. Be wiser to hike it, maybe, stepping from boat to boat all the way to Lake Mead, our destination, 277 miles downstream.

I'm looking for a way to creep off unnoticed when my escape is interdicted by the approach of two of my twenty or so fellow passengers. Some fellows. One is a dark brown exotic wench in a tiger-skin bikini; she has the eyes and hair of Salome. The other is a tall slim trim sloop of a girl with flaxen hair, and elegant sateen thighs emerging from the skimpiest pair of Levi cutoffs I have ever seen. I pause. I hesitate. I reconsider.

Following my bowsprit back to the beach, I join the crowd around Wally Rist, the head boatman, who is demonstrating—on the exotic Salome—the proper way to fasten a life jacket.

Minutes later, all too soon, without adequate spiritual preparation, we are launched forth on the mad and complex waters of the frigid river. John Blaustein, photographer and boatman, has cajoled me into his dory, making certain I do not escape at the last moment.

We pass through the Paria Riffle without upset, much to everyone's relief, as John strains at the oars. Nine years earlier, when I was ranger here, I took my girl friends for rides down these riffles, whacking the waves with a Park Service motorboat. How many propellers did I screw up that summer, pivoting off rocks and driving blindly into unobserved gravel bars? Three or four. (Too much beer, too little bikini.)

A nice little runoff comes in from the Paria River, staining the Colorado a healthy hue of brown. Anything, any color—Day-Glo purple, chartreuse, shocking pink—

is better than the unnatural translucent green, like Gatorade, of our river as it comes strained through the penstocks of that Glen Canyon Dam.

We pass the little beach where, years before, I used to lie on the sand and watch my favorite birds: turkey vultures, shrikes, ruby-throated hummingbirds, rosy-bottomed skinnydippers. Above, on a windswept sun-baked stony bench under the mighty Vermilion Cliffs, is the new Park Service all-metal campground, packed with Winnebagos, house trailers, pickup-campers, trail bikes, jeeps, motorboats, and the other paraphernalia necessary to a holiday in the wilds. Four miles downriver from Lee's Ferry we glide beneath the Navajo Bridge, 467 feet above, which spans the opening to Marble Gorge. As the canyon walls rise on either side of us, a new rock formation appears: the Coconino sandstone.

This is Marble Gorge, entrance to the Grand Canyon. Entering here over a century ago, Major John Wesley Powell wrote as follows in his diary:

August 5, 1869—With some feeling of anxiety we enter a new canyon this morning. We have learned to observe closely the texture of the rock. In softer strata we have a quiet river, in harder we find rapids and falls. Below us are the limestones and hard sandstones which we found in Cataract Canyon. This bodes toil and danger.

Toil and danger. Don't care for the sound of those words. Danger is bad enough; toil is reprehensible. Hope these savage-looking boatmen know what they're doing. They certainly don't look like they know what they're doing. Of course I've been down here before. Used to drive the Park Service motorboat as far as Mile 8, Badger Creek Rapid, and twice went all the way down the canyon on a big motor-driven pontoon boat.

The Kaibab limestone formation rises on either side of us, forming walls that cut off most of the sky. We float through a monstrous defile a thousand feet deep; two thousand feet deep? How deep is the river? one of the passengers asks John. How high are the walls? How fast is the current? The traditional questions. He answers patiently. What's that big blue heronlike bird down there that flies like a pterodactyl? Heron.

John tells us that the Canyon is nearly all rock. How much can you say about rock? It's red here, gray there, it's hard, it's badly eroded, it's a mess. The geol-ogists can't even make up their minds how the Canyon was formed. They once thought it was an entrenched meander, the ancient silt-bearing river grinding down into its bed as the plateau gradually rose beneath it. Now some think it's the result of two rivers, one capturing the other in the vicinity of the present Little Colorado. Old-time geologists spoke of a monster cataclysm. One thing is certain: the Grand Canyon is unique.

Now from up ahead comes the deep toneless vibration of the first major rapid, Badger Creek. The sound resembles that of an approaching freight train on a steel trestle. On the standard scale of 1 to 10 this rapid is rated 4–6. Of intermediate difficulty. Staring, we see the river come to an edge and apparently vanish. Curling waves leap, from time to time, above that edge. Wally Rist, in the leading boat, stands up for a good look, sits down, turns his boat, and facing forward, slides over the glassy rim of water. His boat disappears. He disappears. Two more boats follow. They disappear. Our turn.

"Buckle up," commands John.

We fasten our life jackets. John stands up in the center of the boat, taking his look. Pooled behind the wall of boulders that forms the rapid, the river slows, moving with sluggish ease toward the drop. The roar grows louder. I think of Pittsburgh, the old Forbes Field, seventh game of the 1961 World Series, bottom of the ninth, Yankees leading 8 to 7, two men out, one man on, and the roar that greeted Lou Mazerowski's pennant-winning homer.

Wake up. Daydreaming. John has seated himself, the bow of the dory is sliding down the oily tongue of the rapid, holes and boils and haystack waves exploding all around us. John makes a perfect run straight down the middle. One icy wave reaches up and slaps me in the chest, drenches my belly. *Cold!* The shock of it. But we are through, easy, riding the choppy tailwaves of the rapid. John catches the bottom of the eddy on the right and with a few deft strokes brings our boat to the beach at the mouth of Badger Creek. The other boats join us. Boatmen and passengers clamber ashore. Here we'll make camp for our first night on the river. True, we haven't gone far, but then, we didn't get started till noon.

Setting up camp for the night is a routine chore for the boatmen. All food supplies for the eighteen days, and personal belongings, are neatly packed into the water-tight compartments below the decks of the boats. The large cans of food are packed first, their weight on the bottom of the boat adding stability for the rapids. Next go large waterproof containers with things like bread, eggs, and flour, and army surplus rubber bags for clothing and sleeping gear. Cameras and small personal gear are carried in surplus ammunition cans.

Most of the passengers line up behind the boats to retrieve their rubber bags and immediately disperse up the beach to find a flat spot in the sand on which to set up their camps. There is an ample supply of semiprivate nooks and crannies among the tamarisk trees, so I see no reason to rush, and decide instead to have a cold beer.

One of the boatmen, the one they call Sharky, a fiercely-bearded lad with burning blue eyes, is in charge of toilet facilities. In the old days passengers and crew simply dispersed to the bushes, women upstream, men downstream. Now that the Canyon is so popular, however, with some 15,000 souls per summer riding through, it has become necessary for sanitary and aesthetic reasons to make use of portable chemical toilets. Sharky is our porta-potty porter. He removes the unit from his boat and sets it up among the shady tamarisk far from the beach, in a spot with a pleasant view of the river and canyon walls. He is the kind who thinks of such things. Later, some of the passengers will wander around half the night hunting for it.

The boatmen set up the "stove"—a metal box, filled with dry driftwood and covered with a steel grate. The cooks begin at once preparing supper. Our cooks are two able and handsome young women named Jane and Kenly. Both are competent oarswomen as well, and can substitute for the boatmen if necessary.

Drinking water is taken right from the river, and chemically purified. If the water is extra muddy, lime and alum are added to settle it.

After dinner—pork chops, applesauce, salad, soup, peaches, coffee, tea, etc., the "etc." in my case being a mug of Ron Rico 151—we are subjected to a lecture by Head Boatman Wally. Now that they've taken our money and gotten us down here beyond reach of civilization, he talks about the realities of Grand Canyon life: how to use the portable unit (no simple matter); about cactus, scorpions, centipedes, and "buzzworms" (rattlesnakes); about loose rocks and broken bones, quicksand, whirlpools, and asphyxiation, the remoteness of medical aid. Wally instructs us on what to do if a boat tips over, as it sometimes does; tells us the hazards of diving into the river and swimming in the current.

We pay scant attention to all that rot and soon afterward Sharky digs out his recorder, his ukelele, and his kazoo and announces a porta-potty porter's party. Bottles appear. Darkness settles in, decorum decays. Salome dances in the sand.

One more nip on the Ron Rico and two more songs and then I slink away. I unroll my sleeping bag, but the air is so warm I hardly need to crawl into it. By dawn I will. Two shooting stars trace lingering parabolas of blue fire across the sky. From below rises the sound of rowdy, unseemly music. Crickets chirp. The steady, rhythmic rumble of the river pouring over the rocks is somehow soothing. I soon drop off to sleep.

DAY 2 Another day another dolor.
We wake early in the morning to the sound of Sharky playing his recorder. "Greensleeves," "The Foggy Dew," "Amazing Grace" . . . sweet and simple tunes that float like angelic voices through the great natural echo chamber under the canyon walls. We awake from our dreams into the beautiful dream of day, of wilderness, of the desert.

The troops line up, red-eyed, hung over, but alive, for breakfast. Coffee, fruit juice, apricots, tea, Tang, granola, powdered milk, fresh eggs, bacon, hash browns, it all looks good. After breakfast we pack our bags and load the boats and sit down in the shade to wait for the engineers who operate Glen Canyon Dam to turn our river back on again, to generate enough electricity so those comfort-seeking souls in Phoenix can switch on their lights, plug in their electric coffeepots, toast their bread, dry their hair, vacuum their rugs, air-condition their houses and offices.

Thinking about the dam, I feel a renewal of the wholesome murderous rage that has enlivened my river thoughts for the last sixteen years. Those bloody swine, I'm thinking. Those servile technicians, those corrupt and evil Utah-Arizona politicians, those greed-crazed hogs from the construction companies, those goons and gangsters who boss the unions. We're going to get their stinking dam. We've got secret plans. We're going to set up a laser beam below the dam, drill a tiny hole through the base of it. We've got underground chemists working on the formula for a new kind of acid that will dissolve concrete under water. We have suicide freaks from Stockholm and Tokyo who want to grow up to be human torpedoes, living dive-bombers. We are building the world's biggest houseboat at Wahweap Marina, just above the dam, and filling it with fertilizer and kerosene.

We've hired a muralist from Mexico to paint a jagged fracture down the face of the dam. We've employed a crack team of serious Christians who are praying round the clock for an Act of God. And exorcists from Haiti. Levitationists from the Punjab. Witch doctors from the Congo. Long before it fills with mud, that Glen Canyon Dam is going to go—592,000 tons of concrete aggregate down the river. Your dam is doomed, Mr. Reclamation Commissioner. All is ready but the printed announcements.

Still waiting for the water to rise, we inspect some fossils—nautiloids, crinoids, brachiopods, three-toed lizard tracks embedded in the Hermit Shale, the fourth sedimentary formation in the Canyon. About two hundred million years old. We walk up Badger Canyon to the first jump-off. A rope dangles up there, frayed and gray. Somebody's escape route from the river, years ago.

By noon the water is high enough for boating. We push the dories onto the artificial river, courtesy United States Bureau of "Reclamation," and stroke away. Great blue herons rise before us, flap downriver, find another perch, and wait until we herd them on again. Splendid-looking fowl but stupid. Ravens croak, canyon wrens sing a *glissando*, and in the thickets on the bank we spot a blue grosbeak, an ash-throated flycatcher, a sparrowhawk. John rows and rests. Waterdrops fall from his oars and tinkle on the surface of the placid river. An enormous stillness fills the canyon.

Then the sound of motors. "Baloney boats," says John. We look upstream and see a huge silver-gray rubber raft come charging around the bend, bearing down on us. Swarming with people, it looks like a floating anthill. John pulls our dory aside to let it pass. Waves and shouts. At full throttle the baloney boat roars by. Followed a minute later by a second and a third, all stacked with yellow crates, pink bodies, red fuel tanks. Those passengers sure get a ride—from Lee's Ferry to Lake Mead in as few as six days. The wilderness mass transit system in operation.

The three baloneys skid around the bend below and vanish. Iridescent oil slicks glisten on the water. Gasoline fumes hover on the air, slowly dissipating. Gradually the quiet returns. Nobody says anything for a while. Let them have their hectic joyride in those inflatable Greyhound buses. We, in our oar-powered little dory, are riding in the Mercedes-Benz of rivercraft. Our sense of smug superiority is too assured to require verbal expression. We talk about birds, rocks, rapids, J. Wesley Powell.

August 8, 1869—The limestone of this canyon is often polished, and makes a beautiful marble. The rocks are of many colors—white, gray, pink, and purple, with saffron tints. It is with very great labor that we make progress, meeting with many obstructions. . . .

Ah yes, the rapids. Here they come again. We run Soap Creek Rapid, rated 5–6 on the riverman's scale. Salt Water Wash, where Frank M. Brown was drowned in 1889, surveying for a railroad that was never built. Supai sandstone appears just before we hit Sheer Wall Rapid (2–5). Hot Na Na Wash. House Rock Rapid (4–6). The ratings vary depending on the volume of river flow. Most rapids are easier when the water is high. John runs them all without apparent difficulty.

We hit no rocks but plunge through plenty of waves. Soaked with icy water, burning under the sun, we bail out the boat, gaze up at the towering walls—nearing two thousand feet high at this point—and hurry on, borne forward by the hastening current. In the late afternoon, chilled despite the August heat by the water and the shade of the canyon walls, we are all mighty glad to see Wally's boat pulled ashore on the beach above the mouth of North Canyon. Twenty miles from Lee's Ferry and our second camp. Eight miles yesterday, twelve today. Too fast to suit some of us but better than most do. (The motorized pontoon rafts average thirty to forty miles per day.)

Unloading the dories has become part of a welcome routine. Most of the passengers help out, and scrounge for firewood and carry water. My wife Renée, the tall, slim girl with the legs, has already made herself an integral member of the kitchen crew. Only a few more sensitive types like myself, pained by the sight of toil and turmoil, sneak away for a walk up North Canyon.

You can walk for only a mile or so till you come to an impassable waterfall—dry now—fifty feet high. Below is a small clear pool, evaporating. The silence here, away from the river and the people, is intense. The clash of stone against stone, in the dry air, is harsh, brittle, without resonance or echo. A silence almost supernatural that reminds me of the oppressive stillness in the final scenes of Kubrick's *2001*. I can hear the blood singing in my ears. The sky above, beyond the crooked canyon rim, is a pale metallic blue. Storm coming.

That evening the wind begins to blow. Dark clouds loom, and lightning crackles in the distance. Will it rain? Wally studies the sky. "I can say," he says, "without doubt or qualification, that it might. If not here, somewhere." Renée and I string up our plastic tube tent, supplied by Litton's Dories, Inc., tying one end to a dead arrowweed and the other to a snake. "Hobble that snake." Well, a stick. There's nothing else available. It doesn't rain but all night long the wind howls and the sand swirls in our faces.

DAY 3 Today is a good day. John lets me row his boat. We easily navigate past 24½ Mile Rapid, where Bert Loper, the "Grand Old Man of the Colorado," died in 1949, while rowing himself down the river in celebration of his eightieth birthday. John lets me take the dory through 29 Mile Rapid, rated 4, and the riffle at Mile 30. All goes well at 29 Mile, but at the riffle I barely get around the exposed rock at the head of the chute and am forced to "Powell" the rest of it, stern foremost. Backwards. Like Powell did it. The dory does equally well in either attitude but John is obviously

33

shaken. "Exciting," he says, his knuckles white, "very exciting. Give me back the oars, please."

I thought it was a good run. Any run without loss of boat or passengers is a good run, in my opinion. We pause at Vasey's Paradise for a drink of clear spring water.

August 9, 1869—The river turns sharply to the east and seems enclosed by a wall set with a million brilliant gems. On coming nearer we find fountains bursting from the rock high overhead and the spray in the sunshine forms the gems which bedeck the wall. The rocks are covered with mosses and ferns and many beautiful flowering plants. We name it Vasey's Paradise, in honor of the botanist who traveled with us last year.

Lunch at Redwall Cavern, Mile 33. Lemonade, beer, and avocado-cheese-bean-sprout sandwiches. Excellent. Redwall Cavern is a huge chamber carved out of the limestone by the old predamnation river. Major Powell guessed it would seat fifty thousand people. I'd say five thousand. He was off by a digit but assumed, when writing his celebrated report, that no one else would ever come down the river to check up on him. I'm not calling Powell a liar; Powell is a hero of mine.

But I will say he had a tendency, now and then, as a friend of mine says, to "overexaggerate."

The river, brown before, is taking on a rich red-orange color, *muy Colorado*. Lovely. The good old Paria must be in flood again. So that's where last night's storm was.

We run some modest rapids this afternoon, make third camp at Buck Farm Canyon, Mile 41, early in the evening. Much deer sign—thus the name?—and trickling seeps, emerald pools, tadpoles, red and blue and purple dragonflies, cottonwood, box elder, and the graceful little redbud trees. Back to camp. Soup and salad, steak and sweet corn, plenty of beer for supper. Happiness.

DAY 4 Off again on the river of gold, through a clear bright irreplaceable day. The great Redwall cliffs soaring above, intense and vivid against God's blue sky. Marble Canyon, Powell called this place, though limestone is not marble and he knew it.

At Mile 43, high on the right wall, maybe a thousand feet above the river, we see the remains of some kind of wooden footbridge joining one ledge to the next. Studied through binoculars, the wreckage appears old, very old, the work of Indians. What is it?

Where does it go? Is there a hidden Anasazi granary up there, a concealed pre-Columbian penthouse? I'd like to climb up and see where the bridge leads, if anywhere, but today we have no time for unscheduled stops, we pass on. Next time. I call it Mystery Footbridge in my notes.

We slip through President Harding Rapid (2–4). Onward. Sail on, sail on, oh jaunty dories and your pirate crew, with your cargo of living bodies, sunburned flesh, pothering brains.

We camp tonight at Nankoweap Canyon, Mile 52. The Bright Angel Shale is at river level here. "Nankoweap," Wally explains, "is an old Paiute word meaning 'Place where scorpions crawl into sleeping bags if not detected by unsleeping vigilance.' " Before dinner Renée and I hike up the talus slope under the cliffs to check out the ruins of Anasazi storage structures. Stones and dust; even the ghosts have long since departed.

DAY 5 Onward. We have come only fifty-two miles in four days. We have many miles, many rapids, many more rock formations to go, before this perilous journal is completed.

Kwagunt Rapid (4–6). No problem. 60 Mile Rapid (4). Simple. The Tapeats sandstone appears. We pass the mouth of the Little Colorado River, chocolate-brown with flood waters, and find new and formidable rock formations rising before us. Marble Canyon becomes the Grand Canyon itself. Powell recorded the approach in these words:

August 13, 1869—We are now ready to start on our way down the Great Unknown. We have but a month's rations remaining. We have an unknown distance yet to run, an unknown river to explore. With some eagerness and some anxiety and some misgiving we enter the canyon below. . . .

Dramatic words. Melodramatic, perhaps. And yet with a little effort of the imagination we can understand how Powell and his brave men felt. For two months they'd been battling the river, all the way from Wyoming—upsetting in rapids, wrecking boats, losing supplies, gambling on Powell's belief that a river so silt-laden would not, as rumors had it, disappear underground or trap them between unscalable walls on the verge of a fatal waterfall. Now they were entering the biggest canyon yet, facing the worst rapids, without any sure knowledge of what lay ahead. And low on grub.

Above us on the right stands Chuar Butte. Still visible up there, far above the river, are the aluminum scraps of two big airliners that collided above the Grand Canyon in 1956: 128 went down; all died.

Tanner Rapid, Mile 69. Basalt Canyon, a volcanic region, with grim-looking blue-black cliffs set at a crazy angle to the descending river. We make camp above the roar of Unkar Rapid in the last broad open valley we shall see for the next two hundred miles. Not far downstream the river cuts into the pre-Cambrian gneiss and schists of the upper Granite Gorge, the inner canyon, where the big rapids make their play.

Half-moon in the sky tonight, casting a supernatural glow on the grotesque forms of the Canyon, on the wall known as Palisades of the Desert, on the remote promontory, thirty-five hundred feet above, of Cape Solitude. We can see the tree-lined South Rim, Desert View Tower, and, toward the north, Wotan's Throne.

Found a rattlesnake in the bush. A small one, three rattles, pinkish in color. He looked frightened. We left him alone.

DAY 6 A cool morning, overcast sky. More birds for Renée's list: brown-headed cowbird, western tanager, black-necked stilts, violet-green swallows, black-throated swifts. The swifts like to skim close to the waves in the rapids, attracted, it would seem, by the turbulent air. According to Rich Turner, one of our boatmen, they sometimes hit the waves and drown.

River rising but not high enough. Boatmen nervous about running the serious rapids with insufficient water. Those rocks, those granite fangs foaming with froth in the charging stream. Bad dreams.

We push onto a river the color of bronze, shimmering like hammered metal under the desert sun. Through Unkar—made it! Then 75 Mile Rapid (4–7). Still alive. We pull ashore above Hance Rapid (7–8) for study and consultation.

Hance is always a problem for the dorymen, especially in low water. Just too many goddamned rocks sticking up, or even worse, half-hidden near the surface. No clear route through. A zigzag course. Huge waves, treacherous boils, churning holes that can eat a boat alive. A kind of slalom for oarsmen, with the penalty for a mistake a possible smashed boat. The big advantage of rubber boats is that they can usually be bounced off the well-polished boulders in the rapids without suffering damage. Usually. But rigid crafts likes dories or kayaks may split, puncture, crack like an eggshell. Therefore their safe passage through a big rapid—through any rapid—requires more maneuvering on the part of the boatman. More skill? Let's play it safe and say . . . more *care*. A little more . . . *love*.

The boatmen stand on high points beside the rapid, study the obstacles, consult among themselves. We, the passengers, are herded downriver along the shore by Kenly and Jane, the cooks, and assembled below the rapid. The boatmen are going through this one without us. The boats will be lighter and will draw less water, making them more maneuverable. None of the passengers seem to object to this arrangement. Most of them are busy loading their cameras.

The boatmen run it without us, one by one, not easily but safely. We rejoin our boats. The river carries us swiftly into the Granite Gorge. Like a tunnel of love, there are no shores or beaches in here. The burnished and river-sculptured rocks rise sheer from the water's edge, cutting off all view of the higher cliffs, all of the outer and upper world but a winding column of blue sky. We glide along as in a gigantic millstream. As usual, Powell described the scene as well as anyone ever will:

The gorge is black and narrow below, red and gray and flaring above, with crags and angular projections on the walls. . . . Down in these grand gloomy depths we glide, ever listening, ever watching.

Grand, we'd agree, but not really gloomy. *Glowing* is the word. The afternoon sun is hidden by the narrow walls but indirect light, reflected and refracted by the water, by the pink granitic sills and dikes in the polished cliffs, by the blue lenses of the atmosphere, streams upon us from many angles, all radiant. However, unlike Powell and his men, we are fresh, well fed, well supplied, secure in our bulging life jackets, confident in our dories, too ignorant (except the boatmen) for fear.

Two miles below Hance we crash through the well-named Sockdolager Rapid (5–7), and two and a half miles later into and through Grapevine Rapid (6–7), both so named by Major Powell. Litton's buoyant boats ride high on the waves but not high enough to escape the recoil of the descending 52° waters. Screams of delight, shock, astonishment ring through the canyon as we ride this undulating roller coaster. Unlike the sea, here on the river the water moves, the waves remain in place, waiting for us. Soaked and chilled, we bail out the boats and watch mysterious glenlike tributary canyons pass by on either side. Asbestos Canyon (remains of an old mine up there), Vishnu Creek, Lonetree Canyon,

37

Clear Creek, Zoroaster Canyon, Cremation Creek (what happened there? no one in our party knows), and others. In the early afternoon we pull all seven boats ashore at Phantom Ranch.

Phantom Ranch, combination ranger station and tourist hostel, is the only outpost of civilization within the Canyon. From here broad and well-maintained foot and mule trails lead to both the North and South Rims. Also a telephone line. And a waterline, built at taxpayers' expense, for the motels on the South Rim. There is even a clearing for helicopters. The two footbridges above the river are the only Colorado River crossings from Navajo Bridge to Hoover Dam.

Here we pause for an hour. Some of the passengers are departing us at this point, having contracted for only the first part of the voyage. Their places are taken by others who have hiked the trail down from South Rim. Loaded and ready. One by one the boats shove off, deeper into the inner gorge.

This time my wife and I sit in the bow of the leading dory. Our oarsman is young Rich Turner—musician, philosopher, ornithologist, schoolteacher, rock climber, high diver, veteran oarsman, one of Litton's most experienced hands. Two other passengers are on board: Jane the cook and a newcomer, fifteen-year-old Jenny, a girl from Henderson, Kentucky. Active, athletic Jenny has never been on a river trip of any kind before. As we drift down the river, Rich plying the oars at a leisurely pace, she asks us if we don't get bored sometimes with this effortless mode of travel. Sure we do, but none of us will admit it. We tell her about the birds and the interesting geological formations; the pleasant afternoons in the cool shade, with the sun setting on the high canyon walls; the contrast of the quiet beauty of the side canyons and grottoes with the violent crashing roar of the rapids at the mouth of each side canyon.

Rich suggests that we buckle life jackets. Horn Creek Rapid (7–9) coming up, he reminds us. He says something about The Great Wave. For Jenny's benefit he reviews routine upset procedures: take deep breath when entering rapids; hang on; if boat turns over, get out from under and grab lifeline strung along gunwales; stay on upstream side of boat to avoid being trapped between boat and a hard place; climb up onto bottom of boat as soon as possible; grasp flip line and assist boatman in righting boat; bail out water; relax and enjoy the view.

"What was that about a great wave?" Renée asks.

"I didn't say 'a' great wave," says Rich. "I said '*The* Great Wave.'"

More boatman's hype—short for hyperbole?

Dorymen love to melodramatize the peril of the rapids. Makes their idyllic jobs seem important, gives the gullible passenger the illusion that he's getting his money's worth.

Comes the now familiar growing roar of uproarious waters. Not far ahead the river plays its usual conjuring trick, seeming to pour over the edge of the known world and disappear down into some kind of grumbling abyss. Above the watery rim I can see hints of a rainbow in the mist, backlit by the westering sun. We've seen it before.

What I've forgotten is that Horn, unlike the longer rapids above and below, makes its descent abruptly, in one dive, through a constricted channel where the river is squeezed into sudden acceleration. Rich stands up for a last look but sits down quickly. The boat slides down the glassy tongue of the current. Into a yawning mouth. I take a deep breath—involuntarily. "Hang on!" Rich shouts.

The dory plunges down into the watery hole, then up the slope of the standing wave. Water topples upon us, filling the boat in an instant. The force of the river carries us through the first wave and into a second, deeper hole. "One more!" Rich yells, his oars stroking empty air. We dive into a second wave, taller than the first; it hangs there above my head, a rippling, translucent, liquid wall. Our sluggish boat plows through it.

"And one more!" cries Rich. One more indeed. The dory drops into the deepest hole yet. I think I can almost see bedrock bottom. The third wave towers above us. Far above. The Great Wave. Heavily our water-loaded boat, askew, climbs up its face. Never makes it. As the wave hits us from the portside our dory turns over with the grave, solemn, inevitable certainty of disaster. No one says a word as we go under.

Below the surface all is silent and dark. Part of the current, I do not even feel a sense of motion. But before there is really time to think or feel much about anything, the life jacket brings me to the top. The dory, upside down, is only a stroke away. I grab the lifeline. Renée is hanging on beside me. And Rich and Jenny near the stern, Jane on the other side. The wrong side.

The river carries us swiftly toward the sheer canyon wall below the rapid, on the left. Jane still seems a bit dazed like the rest of us, unaware of her danger. Rich pulls himself onto the flat bottom of the boat and drags her up with him. The boat crunches into the rock. Sound of splintering plywood. The weight of the current forces down the upstream side of the boat, pushing me and Renée underwater again. Down in the darkness I let go of the boat's lifeline and kick away.

39

After what seems an unnecessarily long time I rise to the surface, gasping for air. A wave splashes in my face. Good God I'm drowning, I think, choking on a windpipe full of muddy water. Instinctively I swim toward shore and find myself caught in a big eddy, pulled in a circle by the swirling current. Where's Renée? I see the boat go sailing past, upside down, three people crawling on it, none of them my wife. The eddy carries me close to the wall and I make a futile effort to find a handhold on the glossy, polished stone. I give up and let the eddy carry me down again, toward a tumble of broken rock fallen from the wall. I succeed in getting onto the rocks and stand up, free of the hungry river at last. Renée? I hear her calling me. Ah, there she is, below me on an adjoining shelf of rock. Reunited, we stand on our island in the stream and watch Rich, Jane, Jenny, and the capsized dory float away, getting smaller and smaller. We've forgotten for the moment that there are six other dories still up the river. We are relaxing into a foolish despair, feeling abandoned, when good old John Blaustein—none other!—comes charging through The Great Wave, spots us, rows close enough for rescue. With six soaked passengers aboard, he rows hard after Rich and catches him. Rich is having trouble righting his boat. Not enough weight. John and I assist, pulling on the flip lines, and the boat comes over right side up again. Transfer of bodies, the restoration of our original order.

Rich rows, Renée and Jane and I bail. We open the hatches—not quite watertight after all—and bail them out too. Resting at last, we finally become aware of how chilled we are, through and through. Nobody timed it but we must have been immersed in that frigid water for a considerable spell. Even the sun seems slow in bringing warmth back to our bones.

That evening in camp, as Rich patches up his injured dory with glue and yards of duct tape, it dawns on me why the boatmen sometimes refer to the major rapids as Christian Falls. Why? Because they make a believer out of you.

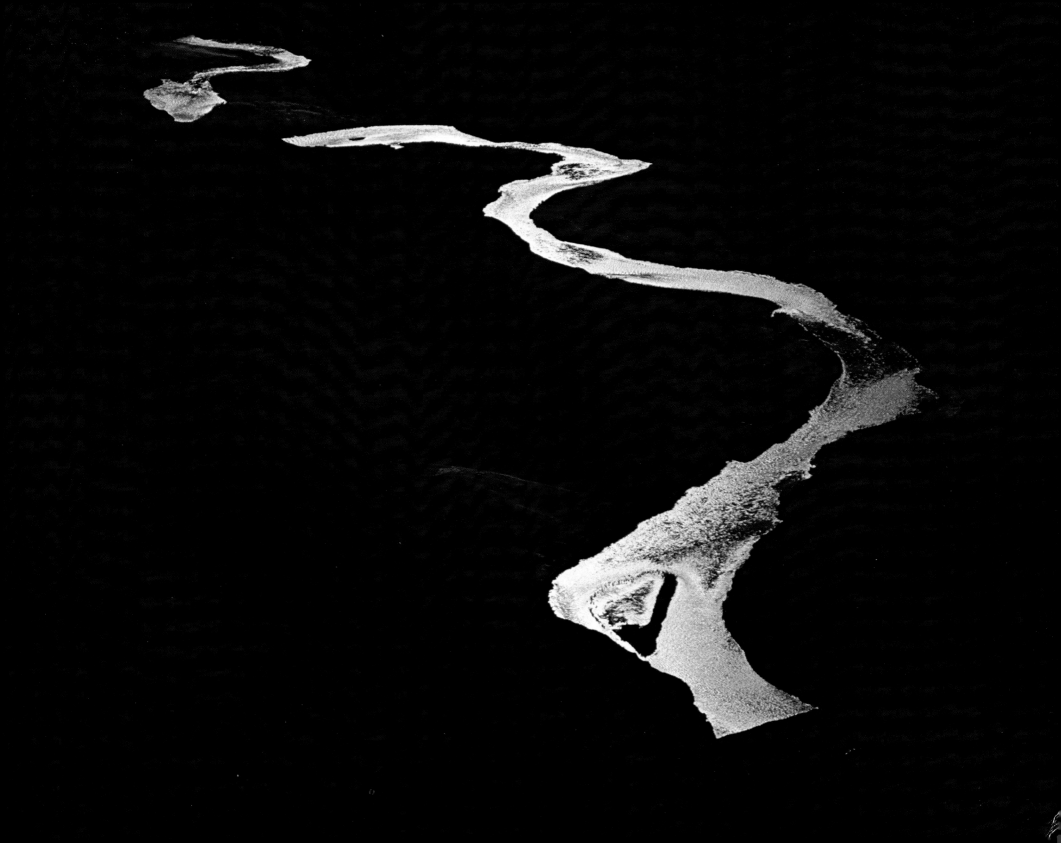

15

17

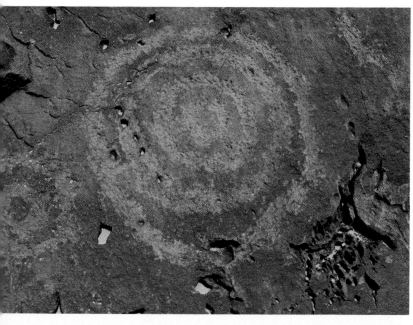

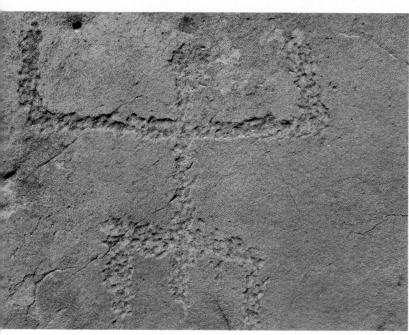

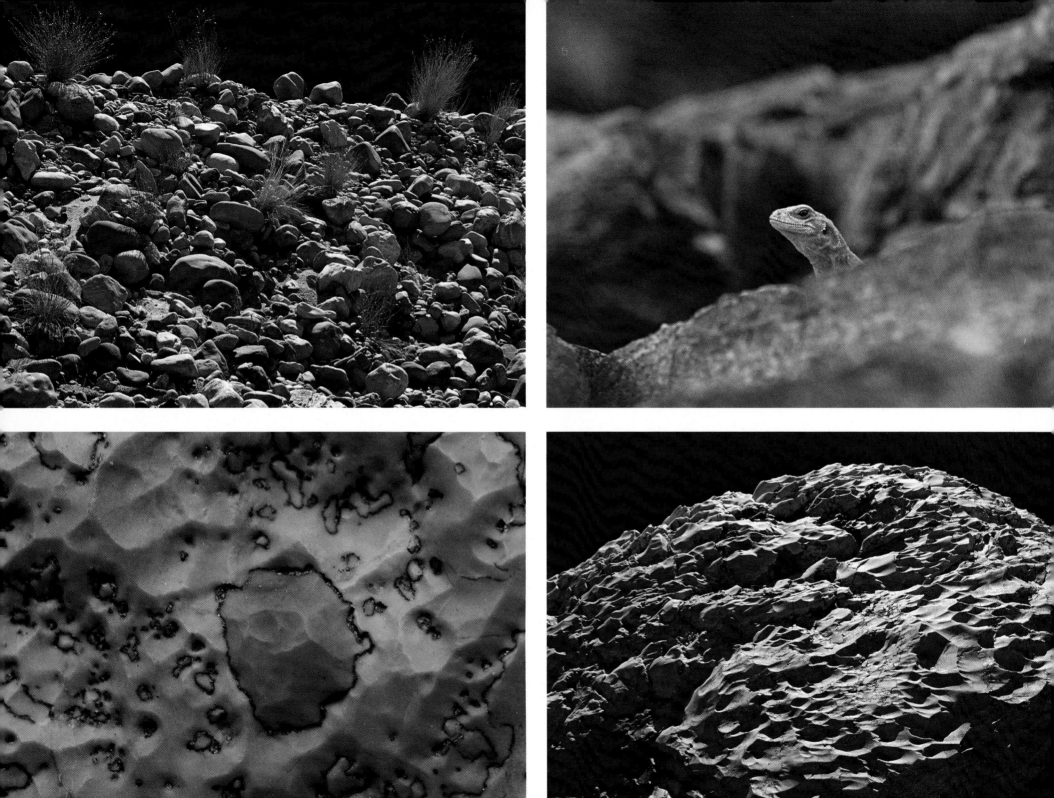

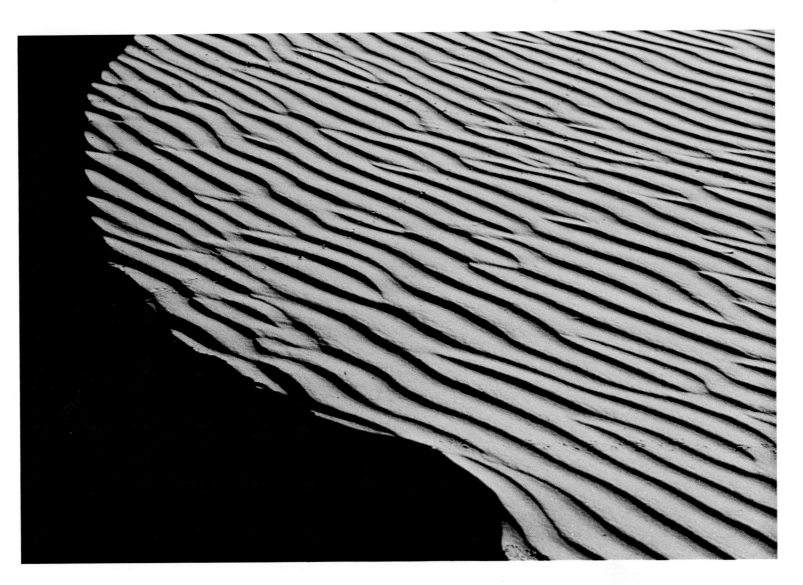

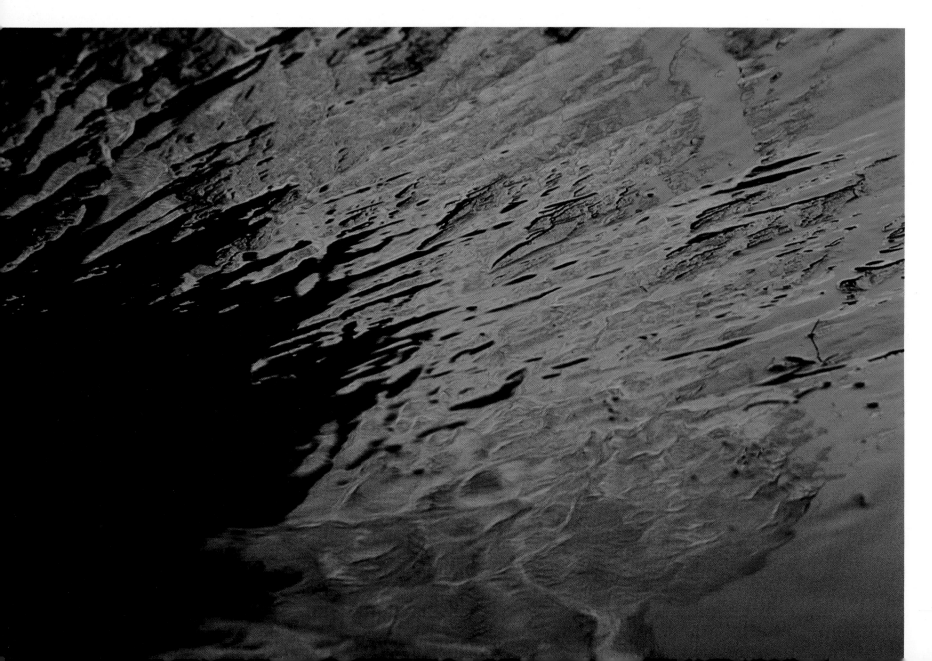

DAY 7 Onward, mates! Drive on, lads! Row on and on, brave dorymen! We have an unknown distance yet to run, an unknown river to explore. I'm beginning to lose track of the days and nights here, my notebook all warped and water-soaked, my pen stove in, my pencils cast to the angry gods of the river.

Today we run a series of hairy rapids, beginning with Granite (7–8). Looks bad but proves an easy run along the right wall. Then Hermit (7–8) and Boucher (4–5). From Boucher I look up and see Point Sublime, far away and far above—six thousand feet above—on the forested North Rim. A place of many sweet memories for me, linked with those summers when I worked as fire lookout up there, in another life, another world. We come to Crystal Rapid (7–10) and all go ashore above it for study and thought.

The boatmen don't like Crystal. Especially in low water, as today. Crystal is a problem, with rocks on the right and a huge churning Eater on the left. Forty feet below lies the Rock Garden, extending all the way across the river except for a narrow channel on each side. So Crystal, like Hance, forms a slalom, an obstacle course requiring some quick maneuvering for a successful run.

As at Hance, the passengers will portage themselves around this rapid. Wally gives his usual big-rapid pep talk: "If you want to see a boat flip, go out of sight. Don't watch us. Go up that canyon there, beyond the bend, and stay there till we're all through the rapid. But if you're for us, stay and yell. We want lots of positive vibrations for this run. We'll need them."

The boatmen start back to their boats. The shutterbugs get out their cameras. We passengers wait, sitting on boulders in the hot sun, surrounded by the unrelenting clamor of the cascading, clashing, tumbling, thundering, tormented waters. Out there in the middle of the maelstrom the Eater waits, heaving and gulping, its mouth like a giant clam's, its roar like the 1896 Republican Convention, its mind a frenzy of beige-colored rabid foam. A horrifying uproar, all things considered. Imagine floating through that nonsense in a life jacket.

A boatman's lot is not (always) an easy one. Is Wally serious about this moral support business? Is he really afraid of secret, unspeakable desires? Telepathic pushes from psychopathic sightseers? Perhaps. I think he's semi-serious. Like a good tour guide he likes to heighten the drama, give the customers an extra thrill. We know that in all the years of commercial river-running through the Grand Canyon—twenty years, a hundred thousand people—only two have died in the river. Others have fallen off cliffs or drowned while swimming, but only two—so far—have been killed directly by the rapids. One was an old lady, smothered when a big rubber raft turned over on her in House Rock Rapid, the other a professional boatman, Shorty Burton, drowned at Upset Rapid (3–8) when his baloney flipped and he was caught in the motor transom rig. You're safer riding a boat or even an inner tube through the Grand Canyon (that's been done) than you are driving your car to work every day for a year. This is what the statistics seem to mean. But despite the odds, despite the proven efficacy of a sound life jacket, there is still something about a big rapid that makes a man nervous. Every time.

The run begins. One by one the dories come through. Wally. Dane. Miltie. Rich. Mike. Sharky. Then John. Only one boatman misses the entry. The others manage to find the narrow slot between the Eater and the rocks on the right side. But Mike, rowing a larger, heavier, aluminum boat, gets a stroke or two behind, is pulled toward the mouth of the Eater and caught by the wave that functions as the Eater's upper lip. The boat is grabbed by that wave, twisted 180 degrees—bow upriver—and tilted on its side. Mike falls out and vanishes into the waves beyond. The boat dances on the monstrous wave like a surfboard, is swallowed by the mouth, then instantly ejected, spat out, and shot downstream. The Eater rejects aluminum! Mike surfaces, swimming around the rocks and into the narrow channel on the right. His boat, miraculously upright and facing properly downriver, bow foremost, sails sedately through the Rock Garden without touching a rock. (Many a tale is told by boatmen, late at night when the passengers are asleep, of unmanned boats making their own way without harm or upset through the most horrendous of gnashing waterfalls.) Mike sees his boat coming, swims to it, climbs aboard. Only the oars are missing, but these are soon found and recovered (each dory carries two spares, just in case). Nobody ever ran Crystal that way before.

After Crystal we pass a series of side canyons with gemlike names: Agate, Sapphire, Turquoise, Ruby. Near Bass Rapid we see an old rusting metal boat stranded high on the left bank, far above the present waterline. Onward, through Shinumo Rapid, 110 Mile Rapid, Hakatai Rapid, and into Waltenberg (3–7). A sleeper. Waltenberg today reveals itself as a tough one—tremendous waves shutting out the sun. We plow through, Renée and I now riding in Mike's big boat. Mike's hands are sore, cut like his knees by rocks from his swim at Crystal. I row his heavy, leaky, water-laden boat the last two miles to our camp at Garnet Canyon. Twenty-one miles today—a record. We are wet, cold, tired, and murderously hungry. Kenly and Jane improvise a hasty dinner and we eat by the light of the waxing moon.

Later, resting on the sand, Mike lays his right hand on a rock and gets stung by a scorpion. A Giant Hairy Desert scorpion, which escapes. Mike doses himself with cortisone and spends a long night hallucinating, aided by the moon, by the stone gargoyles on the canyon rim, and by the image of the Eater gaping wide beneath his dory. Mike's turn; we all have days like that.

DAY 8 In the morning Mike's hand is swollen badly. I row the boat for him from Garnet to Elves Chasm, Mile 116, and from there to our next camp above Blacktail Canyon at the head of Conquistador Aisle, a straight stretch of river three miles long, rare in the otherwise continual turns and twists of the Colorado.

We spend much of the day at Elves Chasm, a magical place with running stream, clear pools, high falls, lush and varied vegetation. Rich does a high dive. All swim. We climb from ledge to ledge, from fall to fall, up pitches of some difficulty. The seven hairy boatmen are there, everywhere, grinning like Bushmen, always ready with a helping hand on wrist, on arm, on thigh or buttock—wherever needed. "A boatman's work is never done," explains Wally, boosting Salome in her mini-bikini up into a rock chimney, where Sharky waits above, teeth gleaming.

We watch the boatmen traverse one ledge with a rather indecent exposure, two hundred feet of vertical space full of nothing but gravity. The ledge is three inches wide. There are no handholds. Most of us choose the sole alternate route, a humiliating crawl on face and belly through a claustrophobic tunnel. No matter. More wonders wait beyond. The route terminates in a kind of amphitheater deep in the cliffs, where warblers sing in the redbud trees and a whispering, shimmering, vaporous veil of crystalline water slips down and down, over moss and algae, past maidenhair fern and helleborine orchid, from the notch in the canyon far above our heads. A breeze caresses the leaves of the willows, hackberrys, box elders. Meditation time.

DAY 9 Drifting down the river after lunch. Riding in Dane's boat now. Sun shimmering in the cloudless sky like a struck and brassy gong. Great balls of fire! and clash of silent symbols. One of the passengers suggests a water fight with the next dory. Dane shudders. "Please," he says, "I hate to get wet. I hate water."

What's this? A boatman who hates to get wet? hates water? Of course. Would you trust a boatman who *likes* water? Beware of lean cooks—and wet boatmen.

Onward and downward. Today we run Forster Rapid (promptly renamed Old Forster) and Fossil Rapid (facile). Then through Specter Rapid, well named for its sinister looming rocks, and Bedrock and Dubendorff. The water is low and the boatmen are concerned about the rocks and waves. There is much going ashore for study, shaking of heads, pointing of hands, debate and council. Like most of the other passengers, I don't understand their technical problems and spend most of my time gazing longingly up the side canyons toward the mysteries of the real wilderness.

Late in the day we land at the mouth of Tapeats Creek, Mile 134. A gravel bar in the middle of the creek prevents us from reaching the campsite on the downriver side of the creek. Because the water between the gravel bar and campsite is shallow enough, we are able to leave the boats on the bar and carry our supplies across the waist-deep water.

DAY **10** Today we hike up Tapeats Canyon and visit one of its tributaries, Thunder River, a great gush of frothy water pouring from a cave in the Redwall. The Redwall limestone formation is full of caverns, partially explored. The whole Kaibab Plateau is full of holes, of which Grand Canyon happens to be merely the most conspicuous.

Half a dozen young nudists from Oakland are camped at Thunder River. The area below the spring looks like it's been trampled by horses. Scarcely a blade of grass or a square foot of undisturbed soil remains. But it wasn't horses. It was people.

All the same, Thunder River is a delightful place. I remember the time a friend and I walked down here from the North Rim, twenty miles in the desert heat of August. Parched as skeletons, we trudged through the heat waves of Surprise Valley (surprise! no shade at all), topped out on a saddle, and looking down, saw these roaring springs, those cool green cottonwood trees, in the middle of the red inferno. Paradise. Of course we'd heard it was here—but we didn't *know* it was here.

A pretty little black and white snake with a white spot on the top of its head, like a caste mark, like a tiny crown, slips across the trail. King snake. It hides deep in the shade of the rocks.

Late in the evening, returning, Renée and I pause on the rim trail high above the mouth of Tapeats Creek and look down at our camp. Shady twilight down in there. Moon rising to the east. Some of the girls are shampooing their hair in the river. Wally and Dane are casting for trout in the creek. Smoke rises slowly, a casual pillar of blue, from the fire. Jenny and Kenly are making a salad. Others lie about reading, dozing, talking, sipping drinks. Murmur of voices. People. Humans more or less, like us, enjoying the ease of a perfect evening, the beauty of a splendid place. And we hear Sharky and Rich with their recorders, playing a duet; the melody of an old, old Shaker hymn floats up toward us on the quiet air:

> *Tis a gift to be simple*
> *Tis a gift to be free*
> *Tis a gift to come down*
> *Where you ought to be. . . .*

DAY **11** The river bears us on. We are leaving Granite Narrows, its tranquil waters, its polished and tortured, embittered and sculpted antique diamond-hard scratch-proof Archean schist. Yes, I'm thinking, it's true, ancient rocks, like old folks, acquire character through endurance of time and adversity, acquire beauty through character. Heraclitus, another riverman, took the words out of my mouth two thousand years ago—"A man's fate is his character. His character is his fate."

Now what? We've run all the really big rapids except the riffle at Mile 179, we've lost nary a soul, we've salvaged several cans of Coors from Beerdrop Falls, we've done Middle Granite Gorge and Thunder River and Deer Creek Falls—

> *August 23, 1869—Just after dinner we pass a stream on the right, which leaps into the Colorado by a direct fall of more than 100 feet, forming a beautiful cascade. On the rocks in the cavelike chamber are ferns, with delicate fronds and enameled stalks. . . .*

Right. At Mile 144, dropping down through Kanab Rapid (2–5), we see a bighorn ram on the left bank. Alone, he paces up and down in a state of mild agitation, as if guarding something, or awaiting somebody. Magnificent beast, proud, erect, alert, bright-eyed, with a full curl to his horns. What a nice trophy his head would make on your rumpus-room wall, oh Mr. Grand-Slammer, you twinkly-eyed mischievous fellow, with your scope-sighted Weatherby 30.06. How about *your* head, properly cleaned and stewed and stuffed, of course, mounted on the canyon wall?

Four miles farther and half a mile up Matkatamiba Canyon one of our party spots more sheep, a half-dozen ewes. Maybe that's what the big fellow was anxious about. We've invaded his turf.

DAY **12** Onward, quickly. Through treacherous Upset Rapid (3–8) where Shorty Burton died, back in '67. We doff headgear in his memory. Going around the bend. Views of Mount Sinyala, above Havasupai country, where the Supai Indians, a small tribe, make their home. The river turns south, west, north, west, and southwest, every which way but loose. We pause for half a day at Havasu Creek.

Blue water, full of travertine. This limestone solution tends to form hard, stony barriers, like little dams, as it flows down the creek to the river. As a result Havasu Creek consists of many falls, cascades, and pools. The pools are deep, clear, and blue as the swimming pools of Phoenix. The falls come in many sizes, including the 200-foot plunge of Mooney Falls, seven miles upstream from the river.

Some of us bear for the big falls but, lured into the luxurious splendor of the blue pools, never make it. We lounge in the limey water, spouting fountains at the sky. It is Wally who broaches the obvious thought: Suppose the world outside—the so-called "real world"—has ceased to exist? Suppose the Bomb has come and gone and we are the sole survivors? For nearly two weeks we haven't seen a newspaper, heard a radio, or smelled the zinc oxide of a TV set; how do we know The World is still out there?

Sobering thought. If it's not, I suggest, then the first thing we'd better do is march up Havasu Canyon to Supai Village and raid the Supai's melon patch.

Sharky shakes his head, looking around at the glistening bodies of the long-haired dolphins splashing gaily in the next pool. No, he says, the first thing we've got to do is start repopulating the earth.

First things first.

Onward, onward. Faster, much faster.

Rowing along from Mile to Mile, nothing to look at but scenic grandeur. Under the lassitude of August, we sink to Sharky's level (might as well, we're in his leaky boat today anyway) and play the word game he calls Hink Pink. Give me a pair of rhyming words, he says, that mean, well, a disappointing disturbance in the course of the river. Pause. Vapid rapid? Right. Two words for small talk about rapids? Riffle piffle? Of course. A dull boatman? Oar bore. A cold river? Rio Frio. And so on. Renée stumps both me and Sharky, however, with this: what is a stitch in time to come?

Long pause. We slide through 164 Mile Rapid (0–1) at the mouth of Tuckup Canyon. Tuckup? Hey, mates, I say, how about this one . . .

Camp at National Canyon (Mile 166)—an inviting spot. All evening long the game goes on; we're incurable. People drift away at our approach, fearing contagion. Worse than Boatman's Rot. Horribly aggravated by Ron Rico 151. Bohemian rowboat? Hip ship. Right. Finally Sharky corners my wife between the fire and the Dutch oven. All right, he says, I give up; what *is* a stitch in time to come? Future suture, says Renée. That's not fair, he says; all hink pinks are supposed to pertain to float trips or boat flips.

Wally talks about safety on the river. Already he's thinking about Mile 179 (Lava Falls—The Big One). Dories are safer than baloney boats, he argues, because they are rigid, won't fold up on you in the rapids. And

71

oars are safer than motors because they're slow, quiet, have no thrashing screw to chop you up if you fall overboard and go under the boat. Dories are safe, he says. *Safer*.

The other dorymen say nothing. They're also thinking about Mile 179. John takes me down to the beach and shows me a rock close to the river's edge. "See this rock?" he says. "That's oracle rock. It tells us the truth about Lava Falls. If the river is up in the morning high enough to cover the rock, we can run the slot in the middle. If the water only covers half the rock, we have a choice. If it doesn't reach the rock at all, we must go right."

"What's the easiest run?"

"The slot in the middle."

"What's the worst?"

"Down the right."

Boatmen and their oracle rocks. Lying on our sacks that night, the old fool moon hanging like a lantern above the black rimrock of the canyon, Rich playing his recorder, Renée and I talk about Mozart, about music, about anything but rocks.

59

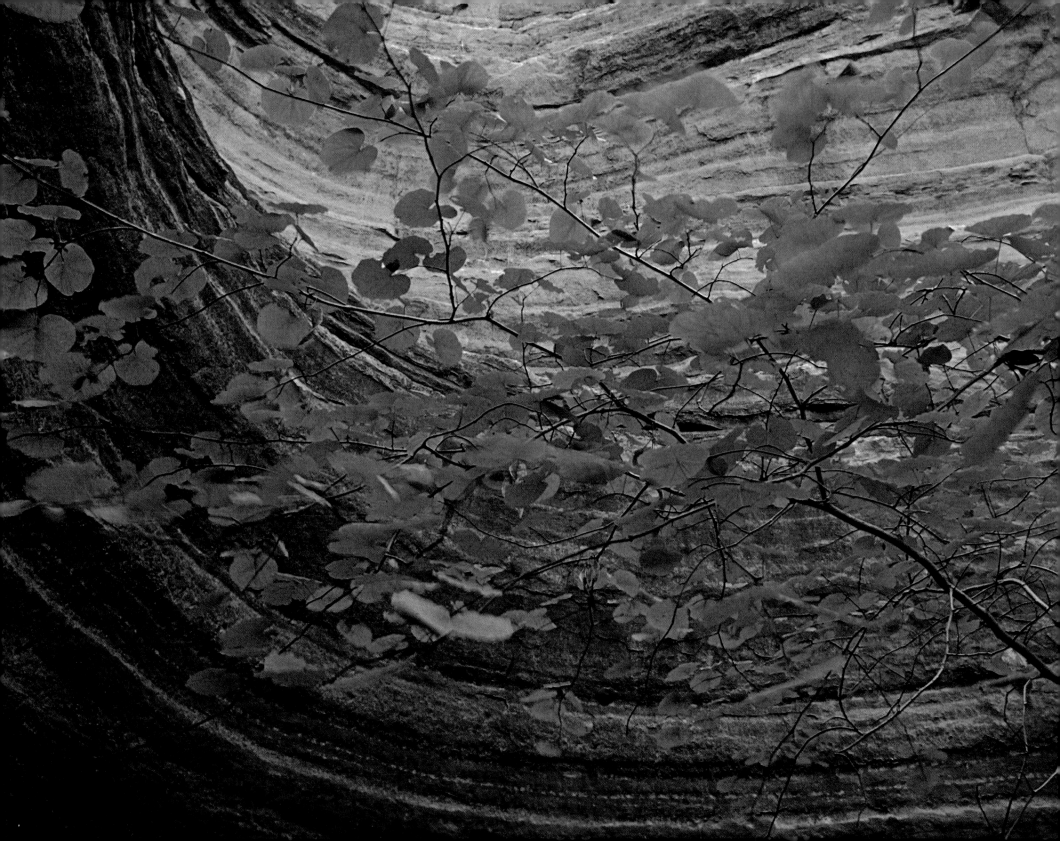

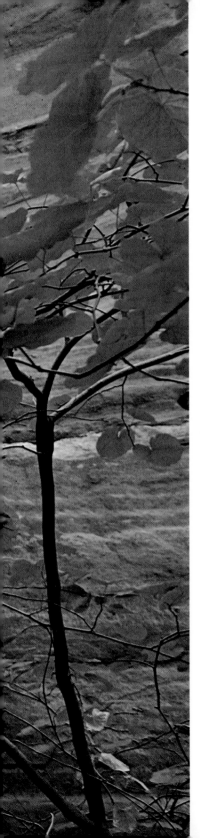

71 / 72

DAY **13** In the morning the river is low. John looks grim. I check the rock. High and dry, and the river dropping slowly.

Breakfast is finished. We load the dories. Some of the boatmen are concerned that their boats are too light, since most of the food is gone. They place large rocks in the bottom of the hatches for ballast. The extra weight down low may help at Mile 179.

August 13, 1869—What falls there are, we know not; what rocks beset the channel, we know not; what walls rise over the river, we know not. . . . The men talk as cheerfully as ever; jests are bandied about freely this morning; but to me the cheer is somber and the jests are ghastly.

Write on, good Major Powell. How prescient you were. I know exactly how you felt. I can read your every emotion on the face of John Blaustein.

We push off. Sunlight sparkles on the laughing wavelets of the master stream. Little birds twitter in the tamarisk.

It looks like a good day to die. All days are good but this one looks better than most.

As Sharky pulls us into the current, lashing about lustily with the oars, I glance back at the beach we are now departing. Only once. A black shadow lies across the unwet rugosities of oracle rock.

The highest sheer walls in the Canyon rear above our heads. Two thousand feet straight up. With terraces and further higher walls beyond. Toroweap Overlook rises at Mile 176, three thousand feet above the river. The suicide's nemesis. We float beneath it.

When I worked at Grand Canyon, a young English major from Yale, unlucky in love, drove his car all the way from New Haven, Connecticut, to jump from Toroweap Overlook. Would have more class, he thought, than the banal routine off Golden Gate Bridge. Arriving here, he took one good look down into our awful chasm ("Gaze not too long into the abyss/Lest the abyss gaze into thee"—F. Nietzsche), walked back to his car (1970 Chevrolet Impala Supersport), attached a vacuum cleaner hose to the tailpipe, ran the other end of the hose into the car, started the motor and gassed himself to death. While gassing he wrote a note explaining his procedure; also a final poem on life, death, and the bitterness of youth that all the critics agreed was not very good. It begins:

I came to Toroweap today

To look, to laugh, to leap away
From all these cares of mortal clay;
I looked—and found a better way. . . .

You see the fatal flaws. Inept alliteration. Heavy-handed rhyme scheme. Iambic tetrameter—wrong foot for elegies. ("Foot like a hand.") Cliché filter not functioning. Sorry lad, you'll have to do better than that. *C minus.*

The river slides seaward in its stony groove. Will never make it. Mohave Desert-type vegetation now—mesquite, ocotillo, catclaw acacia, barrel cactus, clock-face and cow's-tongue prickly pear adore as best they can the talus slopes below the cliffs. Names, names, the naming of the names. What's this? What's that? they ask me, pointing to this bush, that bush. I give my standard reply: What it *is*, ma'am, no one knows; but men call it—creosote bush. *Larrea tridentata.* What's in a name?

We stop for lunch at Mile 177, not far above *that riffle*, from which point we can see the first remnants of the lava flows.

August 25, 1869—What a conflict of water and fire there must have been here! Just imagine a river of molten rock running down into a river of melted snow.

What a seething and boiling of the waters; what clouds of steam rolled into the heavens!

Looking solemn, head boatman Rist gives his final harangue of the trip.

"Listen!" he begins.

We listen. Don't hear a damn thing. Sigh of the river maybe, swooning round the next bend. Cicada keening in the dry grass. Faint scream of the sun, ninety-three million miles above. Nothing significant.

"You don't hear it but it's there," he says. "Lava Falls (ten plus)." Mile 179. "It's always there. Every time we come down this river, there it is. Drops thirty-seven feet in two hundred yards. The greatest rapid in North America. So we're gonna need help from you people. Anybody who's hoping to see a disaster, please stay out of sight. All passengers will walk around this one except volunteers. Yes, we'll need—"

Hands are rising.

"Not yet," Wally says. "We want everybody to see it first. Anybody who thinks he or she wants to ride through Lava has to get down there and walk below it and look up through the waves. Then you decide if you really want to do it. We want people who can handle the oars, who can help right the boat if it flips, and who can climb around on wet boulders if necessary. Nobody has to do it but I'll tell you this much: when you're out there in the middle of Lava, it's nice to hear another heart beating besides your own. *But nobody has to do it*. Nobody has to prove anything—to himself or us. OK? From everybody else, we ask maximum moral support, as before, only more so. After Lava we'll have a party. Any questions?"

Commander Wally's briefing. Tapestry Wally. You'd think we were in a U-boat about to enter a combat zone. Walter Rist—there is something Teutonic about that chap. The straight blond hair. The Nordic nostrils. The sardonic grin. That iron cross, like an amulet, pinned to his life jacket. Yeah, I see through your crude ruse. Nobody has to do it, eh? Not even looking at me he says that. Pretending to talk to everybody but me. Clever, very clever. But you've tipped your hand, Rist. I can read you like the writing on the wall, Wally. No thanks. I glance furtively up and down the river, trapped but not yet panicked. Where is that place? That Separation Canyon? That EXIT from this Hall of Horrors?

Salami on rye, potato salad, peanut butter, and Ry-Krisp for lunch. Not half bad. It's all bad. The condemned man revealed no emotion as he ate his lunch. Ironic laughter in the background. No place to hide. All boats shove off, loaded, onto the shining Colorado. Once more into your britches, friends.

At Mile 178 a great black basaltic rock appears, standing silent in the middle of the river. Vulcan's Anvil, they call it. It looks like a forty-foot tombstone. Staring at it, we hear this weird whimpering noise from midships. Sharky singing his Martian funeral song. Wordless, it rises and falls in hemidemisemitones of unearthly misery. The dirge of the damned.

A muttering sound ahead, beyond the next bend. Wordless voices grumbling in subterranean echo chambers. All boats put ashore on the right bank. Wally leads us, passengers and crew, up a path through the tamarisk jungle and onto a slide of volcanic boulders big as bungalows, high above the river. Lava Falls bellows in the sunlight. He stops. We stop. He waves us on. "Volunteers will assemble here," he shouts, above the tumult from below. "*After* you've looked it over."

We go on, all but the boatmen, who remain clustered around Wally, commencing their customary hopeless confabulations. The sad smiles, the weary headshakings. Same old hype. I smile too, slinking away.

Chuckling, I join the sensible passengers, who gather in a safe shady place near the foot of the uproar. Breathing easily now, I watch these people ready their cameras. Comfortable, we consider the dancing falls, the caldron of colliding superwaves, the lava rocks like iron-blue bicuspids protruding from the foam—here, there, most everywhere, a fiendish distribution of dory-rending fangs. I study the channel on the far left: nothing but teeth. The "slot" in the middle: gone. Hah, I think, they're going to have to run it on the right. Right up against this basalt boxcar I'm relaxing on. Well, serves them right for making such a big deal out of what's advertised as a tax-deductible business trip.

Time passes. Can't see the boatmen from here. I look back up at the "volunteers' " assembly point. Sure enough, a few suckers have showed up, seven or eight of them. And that tall girl in the big hat—my wife? It is my wife. Good Lord, what's she doing there? You can't take my wife. My suture to the future. Who's going to care for me in my dotage, succor my senility? Impossible. They wouldn't dare.

Not all the boatmen are in hiding. John Blaustein crouches on a rock nearby, staring up at the rapids, his battery of cameras dangling from his neck. Like me, he's doing what we're supposed to do: *observe.*

A red, white, and yellow dory appears on the tongue upstream. The Tapestry Wall. There's Captain Wally standing on his seat, one hand shielding his eyes.

He looks pretty, all right, I'll grant you that, heroic as hell. Two passengers with him, sunk deep in their seats, white knuckles clenched on the gunwales. Wally lowers himself into the cockpit, takes a firm grip on the oars. Here they come. They disappear. They emerge, streaming with water. Dive and disappear again. Dark forms barely visible through the foam. The boat rears up into sunlight. Wally has crabbed an oar, lost an oarlock. He's in trouble. He's struggling with something. They vanish again, under the waves, to reappear not twenty feet from where I sit, bearing hard upon this immovable barrier. The dory yaws to port, Wally is standing up, he's only got one oar, looks like he's trying to climb right out of the boat onto my rock. I'm about to offer a futile hand when I realize he's climbing the high side, preventing the boat from capsizing. Cushioned by a roil of water, the boat and its three occupants rush past me, only inches from the iron rock. Who's that lady in the stern, smiling bravely, waving one little brown paw at me? That's no lady, that's my life! Renée. The violent current bears them away, out of sight.

Jesus . . .

One made it. Six more to go. We have to sit and watch this? Too late now, here comes Dane Mensik at the control console of the *Vale of Rhondda*. A passenger in the bow. He makes a perfect run, bow first through the holes, over the big waves, and clears Death Rock by a safe and sane three feet. And after him Mike "Miltie" Davis in the *Music Temple*. Likewise, a perfect run.

Three safely past, four to go. Now come in quick succession Sharky Cornell ("You saw it first in the *Columbia*, folks"), Mike "Scorpion" Markovich in the big *Moqui Steps* (his good right hand no longer numb), and Rich Turner in the patched-up *Celilo Falls*. With a light payload of ballast—one passenger each—they make it right side up, one way or the other way, through the sound and the fury of Mile 179.

Thank God . . .

Only one to go. Poor old John Blaustein in the (ill-named) *Peace River*. I glance up at the volunteers' assembly point. The slave block. One little girl stands there clutching her life jacket, hopefully waiting. No, it can't be. Yes it is, it's Jenny, the kid who changed our luck at Horn Creek. The innocent Jonah. Now I really feel sorry for John. Not only are the scales of probability weighing against him—for if six made it through, the seventh is doomed for certain—but he and he alone has to ride with that sweet little jinx we picked up at Phantom Ranch. Tough luck, John. Kismet, you know. Bad karma. (But better him than me.)

Where is John by the way?

I feel a firm hand on my shoulder. "Let's go," he says.

Well, of course I knew it would turn out like this all along. I never had a chance.

We trudge up the rocks, pick up Jenny, trudge through the jungle and down to the lonely boat, hyperventilating all the way. Buckle up. John gives stern instructions, which I don't hear. Push off. Me and little Jenny in the bow. The sun glares at us over the oily water, blazing in our eyes. John points the boat the wrong way, right down the tongue into the heart of the madness. The moment of total commitment. This is absurd. We dive head first into the absurdity . . .

Twenty seconds and it's all over. Twenty seconds of total truth and then we're cruising through the tail of the rapid, busy with the bailers, joining the procession of dories before us. Nothing to it. Like I always say, running the big rapids is like sex: half the fun is in the anticipation. Two-thirds of the thrill is in the approach. The remainder is only ecstasy—or darkness.

On the beach. The moon is shining bright. The boatmen, armed with heavy grog, are having a private "debriefing" session downstream somewhere. Lewd sil-

houettes prance before our fire. Salome dances. The Abbeys dance. Inhibitions fall like dandruff. Our four French passengers are finally speaking with our two Austrian passengers. (Dieter and his daughter—ah, there's a story.) The others—a twenty-three-year-old schoolteacher; a newspaper publisher, his wife, and three kids; a stockbroker; a retired lawyer; a dental hygienist; a physician—go over the exciting events of the day. No one seems to be able to agree on what happened exactly during those twenty seconds in Lava Falls. No matter; we made it alive. That's what counts.

Dinner is served, vaguely. The seven merry boatmen stagger up from the lower beach, smiling and content. The sense of exhilaration and victory lasts all through the night, waning only with the sunrise.

DAYS **14-18** For yes, we've got a hundred miles yet to go. A hundred miles from Lava Falls to Pierce Ferry on Lake Mead before this voyage is done. There's the Lower Granite Gorge with all its gorgeous sculptured stone. There's Requiem Rapid (4–7) where Mr. and Mrs. Hyde were lost in 1928, never to be seen again. There's 234 Mile Rapid where James Ervin escaped from the Canyon in 1931; his partner was never found. There's Bridge Canyon at Mile 235 where the eager beavers from Reclamation *still* hope to build another dam. There's Separation Canyon at Mile 239½ where three of Powell's men left him, in sad farewell, and climbed out of the Canyon, and never were seen again. There's Lava Cliff Canyon and Travertine Grotto and Burnt Canyon and Tincanebitts Canyon and Bat Cave and Emery Falls and Travertine Bluff and Grapevine Wash. And the Grand Wash Cliffs surmounting all the open country to the west, the terminus of the Canyon. Great place for rolling rocks. And the long row across Lake Mead against the wind to the dismal shores of Pierce Ferry. . . .

Yes, the river goes on and on but the telling of it, unlike the running, becomes wearisome and I am going to end this journey soon. I am going to end it where we began, near Lee's Ferry and *that dam*, making it semicircular.

I want my tale, like our river, to go on to the sea and rise with the sea in mighty clouds, to ride the west winds back to the source in the Rockies once again, over and over and over again. The river is linear but its course is the lazy figure eight of infinity. Finite but unbounded. I want my story to be like a hoop snake, rolling along with its tail in its mouth.

My tale tapers to a death rattle, beware! don't tread on me! For we are going to have our river whole again, someday soon. Glen Canyon was part of our river before and shall be again. Glen Canyon, though different, was equal in its marvels to the Grand Canyon. And the whole river once again, from its confluence with the Green to its effluence in Lake Mead, shall be the property of the American people. Of the world's people. Of the king snake and the rattlesnake, the golden eagle and canyon wren, the coyote, lion, kit fox, mule deer, bighorn sheep, and pronghorn antelope. Glen Canyon Dam must fall. Must soon come tumbling down. All old river rats dead and gone and yet to come will understand. The spirit of John Wesley Powell will understand, high in his haunt on the rim of Great Thumb Mesa. Listen to his words, still whispered by the wind:

We have an unknown distance yet to run
An unknown river to explore

Night and day the river flows. If time is the mind of space, the Colorado is the soul of the desert. Brave boatmen come, they go, they die, the voyage flows on forever. We are all canyoneers. We are all passengers on this little living mossy ship, this delicate dory sailing round the sun that humans call the earth.

Joy, shipmates, joy.

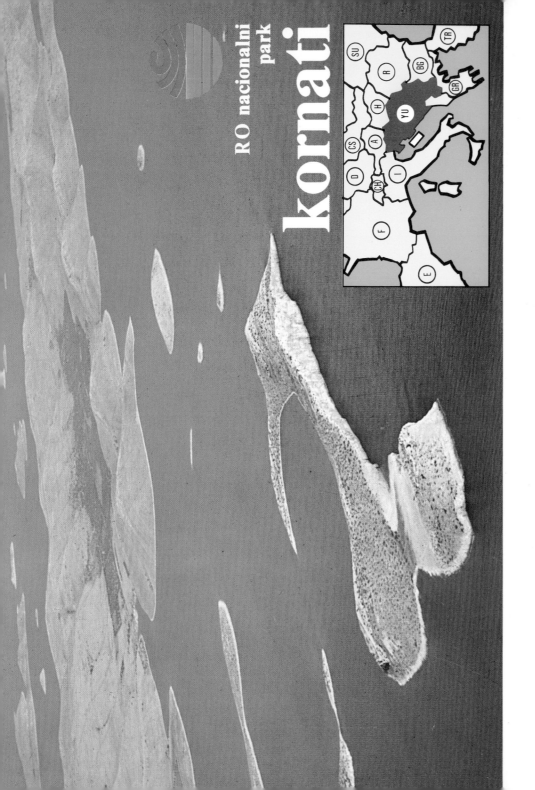

RO nacionalni park
kornati

Turističke informacije:

- Svakodnevni polasci brodom iz Murtera u NP »Kornati«
- Razgledavanje podmorja specijalnim brodom
- Noćno razgledavanje podmorja i krstarenje po NP
- Planinarska staza »Kornati«
- Piknik centar na otoku Levrnaka
- Restaurant »Žakan«
- Marina »Panitula«
- Program robinzonskog odmora

Nacionalni park Kornati

Vodič:
Kornatsko otočje proglašeno je nacionalnim parkom 1980. godine i spada u neponovljiva čuda prirode. Nacionalni park »Kornati« je jedinstvena otočna skupina ne samo na Jadranu, nego i na cijelom Mediteranu. Na površini od cca 240 km² nalazi se 101 otok i otočić. Krajolici i panorama koji proizlaze iz njihove razvedenosti, specifični su i jedinstveni, Kornati su zanimljivi i po tome što predstavljaju najveću površinu na našoj obali bez stalne naseljenosti.
Nacionalni park »Kornati« pored pejsažnih vrijednosti obiluje geomorfološkim lokalitetima, tragovima grčke, ilirske, rimske i staroslavenske kulture, te značajnim lokalitetima iz NOB-a.

Touristische Informationen

- Täglicher Schiffsverkehr von Murter zum Nationalpark »Kornati«.
- Besichtigung des Meeresgrunds mit spezialen Booten
- Nächtliche Besichtigung des Meeresgrunds und Kreuzfahrt durch den Nationalpark
- Bergsteigerweg »Kornati«
- Picknickzentrum auf der Insel Levrnaka
- Restaurant »Žakan«
- Marina »Panitula«
- Programm einer Robinsonade

Nationalpark Kornati

Reiseführer:
Die Inseln Kornati wurden im Jahre 1980 zum Nationalpark ernannt und zählen zu den unwiederholbaren Wundern der Natur. Der Nationalpark »Kornati« ist eine einzigartige Inselgruppe, nicht nur in Adria, sondern in ganzem Mittelmeer. Auf einer Oberfläche von ca. 240 km² befinden sich 101 Inseln und Inselchen. Die durch ihre gegliederte Küste gebildete Landschaft und das Panorama sind spezifisch und einzigartig. Die Inseln Kornati sind auch deswegen interessant, weil sie die grösste Oberfläche auf unserer Küste ohne fester Bevölkerung darstellen.
Der Nationalpark »Kornati« besitzt neben landschaftlicher Werte auch viele geomorphologische Lokalitäten, Spuren der griechischen, illyrischen, römischen und altslawischen Kultur, sowie bedeutende Lokalitäten aus der Volksbefreiungskan.

Informazioni turistiche:

- Partenze cotidiane in battello da Murter al PN »Kornati«.
- Osservazione del mondo subacqueo dal battello speciale
- Osservazione notturna del mondo subacqueo e crociera nel PN »Kornati«
- Sentiero alpinistico »Kornati«
- Centro di picnic sulla isola Levrnaka
- Ristorante »Žakan«
- Porto di diporto »Panitula«
- Programma di riposo nel stile di Robinson Crusoe

Parco Nazionale »Kornati«

Guida:
Le isole Kornati sono proclamate parco nazionale nel 1980 e fanno parte delle meraviglie naturali irreperibili. Il parco nazionale Kornati è un gruppo unico delle isole non solo sull'Adriatico ma anche su tutto il Mediterraneo coprendo una superficie di circa 240 km con 101 isole i isolotti. I paesaggi ed il panorama che derivano dalla loro costa articolata sono specifici e straordinari. Kornati sono pure interessanti perchè comprendono la più grande area della ns. costa senza abitanti permanenti. Oltre le bellezze panoramiche il parco nazionale Kornati è ricco di località geomorfologiche, tracce di cultura greca, illirica, romana e paleoslava, come pure di località importanti nella Lotta di liberazione popolare.

Turist information:

- Daily departures of ships from Murter to the Kornati NP
- Excursions by a special ship to observe underwater life
- Observation of underwater life at night and cruising in the NP
- The Kornati mountain path
- A picnic center on the Levrnaka Island
- The Žakan Restaurant
- The Panitula Marina
- Program of a Robinson style vacation

National park »Kornati«

Guide:
The islands of Kornati were proclaimed a national park in 1980 and are considere as one of the unrepeatable miracles of the nature. The National Park »Kornati« covers a unique group of islands, not only in the Adriatic sea but also on the whole of the Mediterranean, where on a surface of about 240 square kilometers there are 101 bigger and smaller islands. Landscapes and panorama owning to the abundance of their natural forms are exceptional and unique. They are interesting also as the largest area on our coast without permanent population.
In addition to these beautiful landscapes the National Park »Kornati« is rich with geomorphological localities, traces of Greek, Illyrian, Roman and Old-Slavic cultures, as well as with important places from the time of the National Revolution during the Second World War.

Adresa: RO Nacionalni park »Kornati«, 59243 Murter, Matije Gupca 2, Yugoslavia Tel. (059) 75-058

VII/88

Interpublic

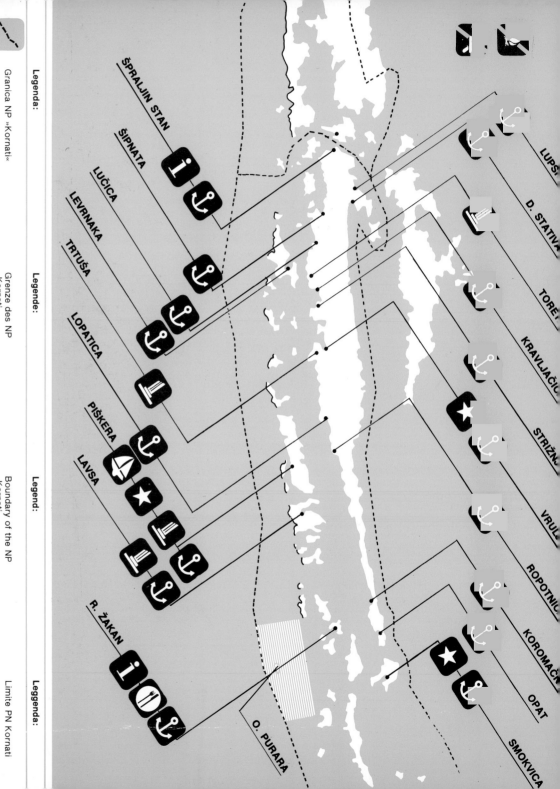

Legenda:

Symbol	Hrvatski	Deutsch	English	Italiano
— — —	Granica NP »Kornati«	Grenze des NP »Kornati«	Boundary of the NP »Kornati«	Limite PN Kornati
	Zona posebne zaštite	Das besonders geschützte Gebiet	The zone for particularly protection	Zona particolarmente protetta
⚓	Sidrište	Ankerplatz	Anchorage	Ancoraggio
ℹ	Informacije Recepcija	Information Rezeption	Information Reception	Informazioni Ricezione
★	Spomenici NOB-a	Denkmäler aus Volksbefreiungskampf	Monuments of the National Revolution	Monumenti della Lotta di liberazione popolare
	Povijesno kulturne znamenitosti	Historisch-kulturelle Sehenswürdigkeiten	Historical and cultural places	Curiosità culturali ed istoriche
	Restaurant	Restaurant	Restaurant	Ristorante
	Klifovi	Felswände	Kliffs	Rocce
	Marina	Marine	Marine	Marina

Pravila ponašanja u Nacionalnom parku »Kornati«

- Za kretanje unutar Nacionalnog parka svi posjetioci moraju imati ulaznicu.
- Na području Nacionalnog parka noćno sidrenje je dozvoljeno jedino u naznačenim sidrištima.
- Zabranjeno je zagađivanje mora i onečišćavanje područja Nacionalnog parka.
- Smeća se odlaže na javna odlagališta.
- U zoni posebne zaštite zabranjuje se svaka aktivnost na moru i kopnu. Na tom području zabranjuje se kretanje posjetioca bez pratnje nadzornika.
- Za ribolov se mora se imati dozvola Uprave Nacionalnog parka.

Hinweise für das Verhalten im Nationalpark »Kornati«

- Innerhalb des Nationalparkes sollen alle Besucher eine Eintrittskarte besitzen.
- Auf dem Gebiete des Nationalparkes ist die Nachtverankerung nur auf den bezeichneten Ankerplätzen erlaubt.
- Meeresunreinigung und Verschmutzung des Nationalparkes sind verboten.
- Die Müllabladung erfolgt auf öffentliche Müllabladeplätze.
- In der Zone des besonderen Schutzes wird jede tätigkeitsform am Meer wie auch am Festland verboten. Auf diesem Gebiet ist das Besichtigung ohne Begleitung des Aufsehers nicht erlaubt.
- Für den Fischfang ist ein Fischerschein von Nationalparkverwaltung erforderlich.

Regole di condotta nel Parco nazionale »Kornati«

- Nel Parco nazionale tutti i visitatori devono avere il biglietto.
- Sul territorio del Parco nazionale è permesso l'ancoraggio di notte solo sugli ancoraggi marcati.
- È vietato inquinare il mare e sporcare il territorio del Parco nazionale.
- Le spazzature bisogna deporre negli immondezzai pubblici.
- Nella zona di protezione speciale è vietata ogni attività al mare e per terra. In questa zona è vietata la circolazione dei visitatori non accompagnati dalle persone autorizzate.
- Per la pesca bisogna avere il permesso della Direzione del Parco nazionale.

Rules of behaviour in the National Park »Kornati«:

- Only the visitors with tickets are allowed to circulate in the area of the National Park.
- Anchoring for night is allowed in the area of the National Park on the marked anchorages only.
- It is forbidden to pollute the sea or to contaminate in any way the area of the National Park.
- Garbage is to be disposed on public rubbisch-heaps.
- In the district of special protection, any activity on the sea or on the land is forbidden. The visitors are not allowed to move about in the district if not accompanied by the supervisor.
- For fishing a fishing licence from the National Park Management is required.

88

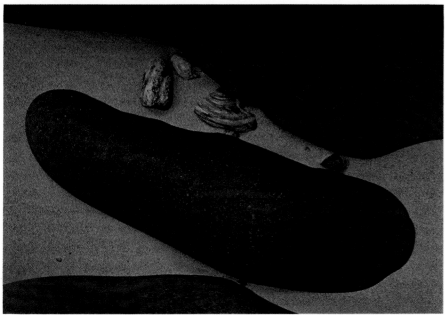

89
90

91

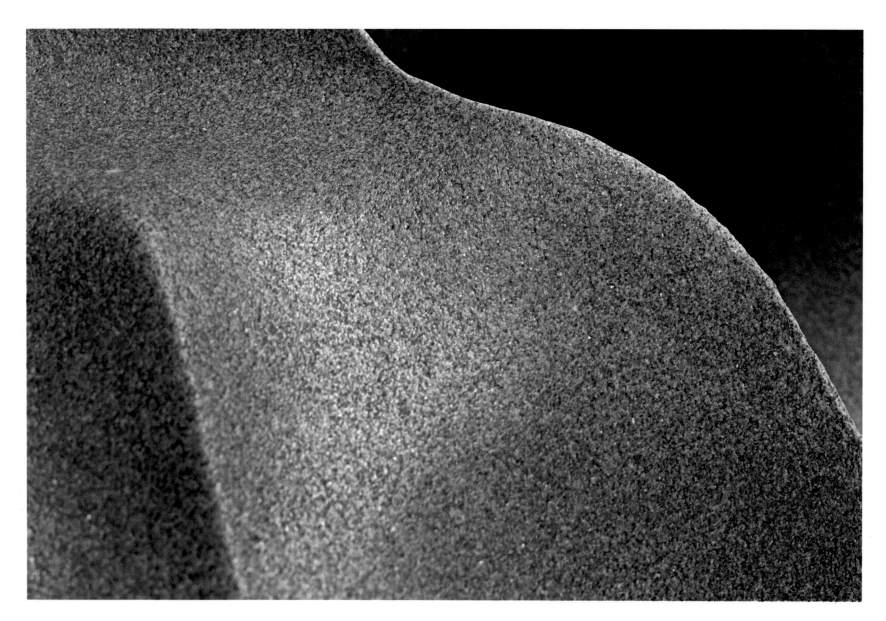

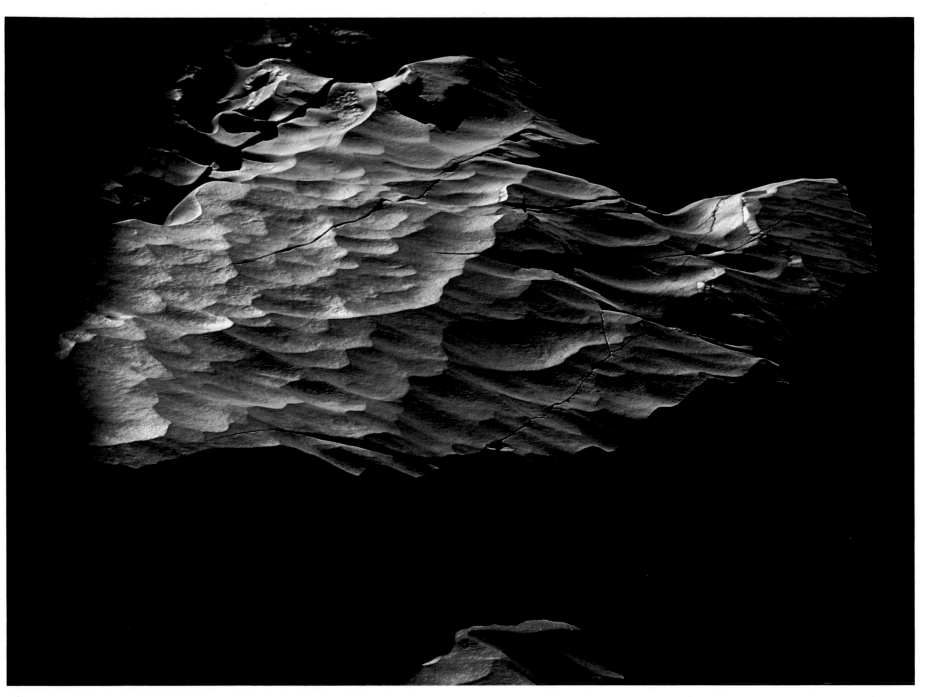

GEOLOGICAL TABLE

ROCK FORMATION	APPROXIMATE AGE IN MILLIONS OF YEARS	PERIOD	ERA
Kaibab Limestone	250		
Toroweap Limestone	255		
Coconino Sandstone	260	Permian	
Hermit Shale	265		
Supai Sandstone	285	Pennsylvanian	Paleozoic
Redwall Limestone	335	Mississippian	
Temple Butte Limestone	355	Devonian	
Muav Limestone	515		
Bright Angel Shale	530	Cambrian	
Tapeats Sandstone	545		
Grand Canyon Series	1200		
Zoroaster Granite	1600		Precambrian
Brahma and Vishnu Schist	2000		

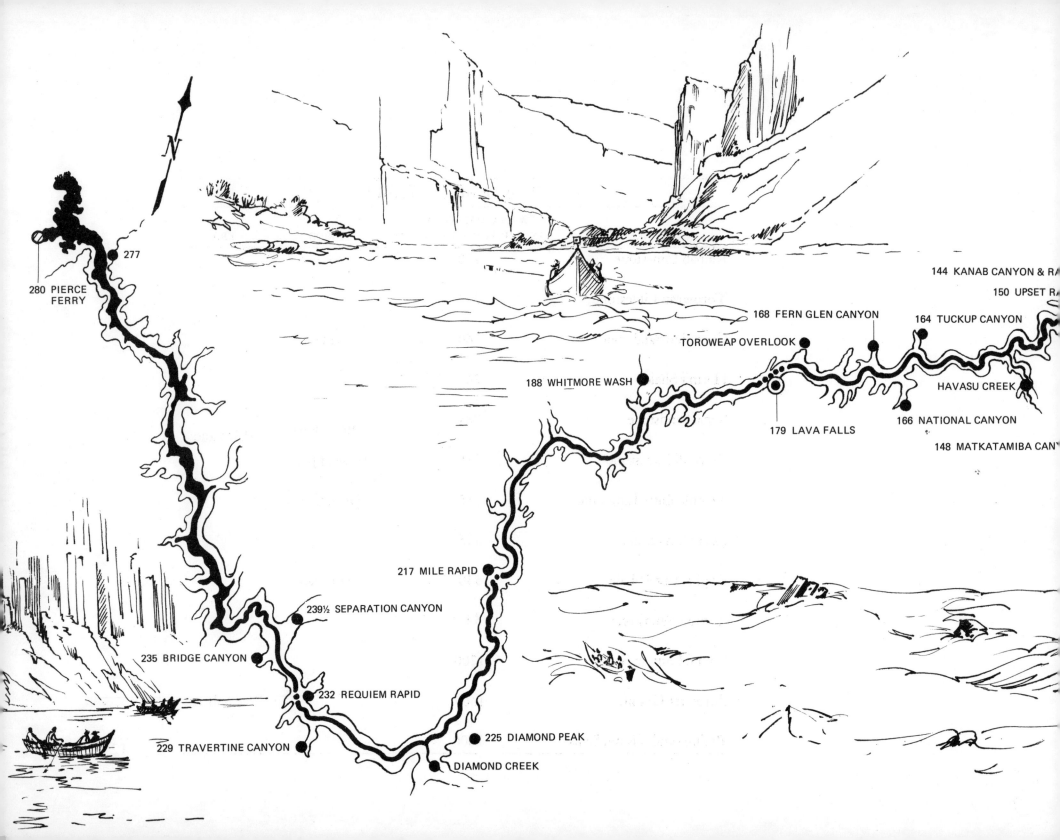

280 PIERCE FERRY

277

144 KANAB CANYON & RA

150 UPSET R

168 FERN GLEN CANYON

164 TUCKUP CANYON

TOROWEAP OVERLOOK

188 WHITMORE WASH

HAVASU CREEK

166 NATIONAL CANYON

179 LAVA FALLS

148 MATKATAMIBA CAN

217 MILE RAPID

239½ SEPARATION CANYON

235 BRIDGE CANYON

232 REQUIEM RAPID

229 TRAVERTINE CANYON

225 DIAMOND PEAK

DIAMOND CREEK

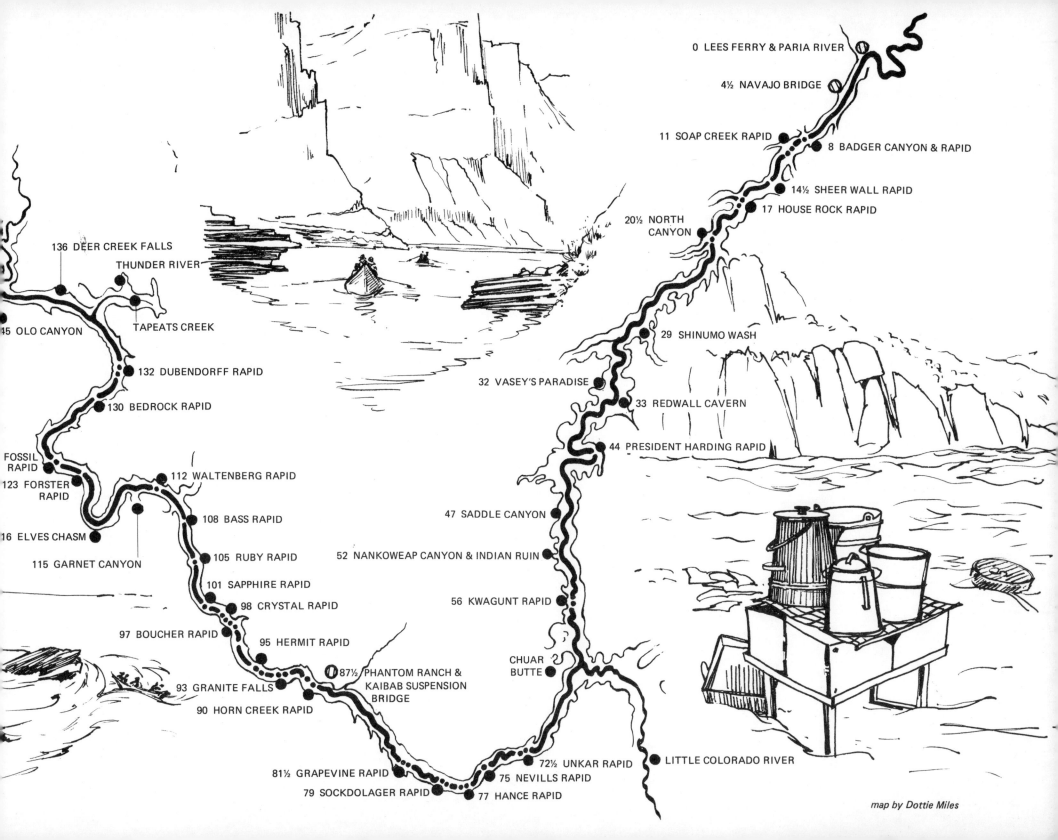

0 LEES FERRY & PARIA RIVER

4½ NAVAJO BRIDGE

11 SOAP CREEK RAPID

8 BADGER CANYON & RAPID

14½ SHEER WALL RAPID

17 HOUSE ROCK RAPID

20½ NORTH CANYON

29 SHINUMO WASH

32 VASEY'S PARADISE

33 REDWALL CAVERN

44 PRESIDENT HARDING RAPID

47 SADDLE CANYON

52 NANKOWEAP CANYON & INDIAN RUIN

56 KWAGUNT RAPID

CHUAR BUTTE

LITTLE COLORADO RIVER

72½ UNKAR RAPID

75 NEVILLS RAPID

77 HANCE RAPID

79 SOCKDOLAGER RAPID

81½ GRAPEVINE RAPID

87½ PHANTOM RANCH & KAIBAB SUSPENSION BRIDGE

90 HORN CREEK RAPID

93 GRANITE FALLS

95 HERMIT RAPID

97 BOUCHER RAPID

98 CRYSTAL RAPID

101 SAPPHIRE RAPID

105 RUBY RAPID

115 GARNET CANYON

116 ELVES CHASM

108 BASS RAPID

112 WALTENBERG RAPID

123 FORSTER RAPID

FOSSIL RAPID

130 BEDROCK RAPID

132 DUBENDORFF RAPID

145 OLO CANYON

TAPEATS CREEK

136 DEER CREEK FALLS

THUNDER RIVER

map by Dottie Miles

Notes to the Plates

1. Mile 202. Lightning during a summer thunderstorm. This picture was taken in the middle of the night by placing the camera on a tripod and opening the shutter until the lightning flashed. The foreground is illuminated by additional flashes above and behind the camera. I was able to watch the dazzling show from the inside of a cave.

2 & 5. Mile 33. Violent thunderstorm flooding, photographed from within Redwall Cavern. Runoff, caused by thunderstorms such as this, is one of the main forces of erosion at work in the Grand Canyon. Water, carrying rocks and dirt, has cut the side canyons and moved the debris into the river. Rapids are formed at the mouths of the side canyons by boulders washed into the river.

3. Mile 202. Thunderclouds accumulate during the storm.

4. Mile 155. Heavy rain falling on the river, photographed from under a limestone ledge.

6. Mile 178. Early morning upstream view from Toroweap Overlook, twenty-seven hundred feet above the river.

7. Last bit of daylight on the Canyon wall, photographed from the South Rim. Unkar Rapid, Mile 72½, is just hidden from view in the bend of the river (left).

8. Sunset from Toroweap Overlook. Lava Falls looks like a small white riffle from this distance.

9. The early morning sun reflected on the river just above Unkar Rapid in the Great Unconformity, near Mile 72. The picture was taken from an airplane with a medium telephoto lens.

10. Mile 8. Badger Rapid (4–6), at the mouth of Badger Canyon (on the right) and Jackass Canyon (on the left). Notice the chocolate brown runoff flowing into the river from Jackass Creek. The clear water, issuing from Glen Canyon Dam twenty-three miles upstream, is stained by the very small amount of muddy water with which it mixes. Boatmen run Badger down the middle of the slick green tongue at the top of the rapid.

11. A dory approaching the tongue of Badger Rapid. The boatman steers his craft sideways, against the current, so he can make position adjustments to the left or the right just before entering the rapid. Note that the boat carries two spare oars, one of which can easily be grabbed and put into the oarlock within seconds should it be needed.

12–15. Mile 11. Running Soap Creek Rapid (5–6). Though the boatman is supposed to hit the waves head-on, my boat was turned sideways and I was almost washed out by the big waves. Fortunately I didn't fall out, but instead regained control for the rest of the rapid.

16. "Rock sculpture" in the Supai formation, photographed from the boat just below Sheer Wall Rapid.

17. Mile 20½. A pool carved into the Supai formation about a mile from the river up North Canyon.

18. Snowy egrets on a beach in Marble Canyon.

19. Mile 32. Vasey's Paradise, a spring flowing from the Redwall limestone formation. Major Powell named this spot after a botanist friend who was never to see it.

20 & 21. Mile 33. Redwall Cavern, a cave carved into the Redwall limestone formation in Marble Canyon. Major Powell described the cavern as "a vast half-circular chamber which, if utilized for a theatre, would give seating to 50,000 people."

22. Mile 34. One of the great pleasures of a trip down the Colorado: floating beneath the vertical walls of Marble Canyon in the late afternoon.

23. Moonrise over the Redwall limestone formation.

24. Mile 44. The river at sunrise, looking downstream from below President Harding Rapid.

25. Mile 42. Just below Buck Farm Canyon. I photographed the buck with a 200-mm. lens at 1/60th of a second from the boat as we quietly drifted by, barely noticed.

26. Mile 52. The Nankoweap Indian ruin, approximately five to six hundred feet above the river. These structures, built by the Anasazi over eight hundred years ago, served as storage graineries.

133

27 & 28. Anasazi petroglyphs near South Canyon, Mile 31½.

29. Mile 52. The view downstream from near the Indian ruin at sunset. One often wonders why the Indians built the structures so far from the river—this view might have been reason enough.

30. Mile 52. A boulder bar, composed of rocks deposited by the river, forms the riverbank.

31. A chuckwalla, tentatively surveying the scene before leaving the safety of his rock hideout.

32. Detail of a limestone boulder. The reddish inclusion in the center is about one inch in diameter. Photographed with a micro lens.

33. A limestone boulder with fluting. The river, heavily laden with silt, carved these razor-sharp edges into the rock. The silt now collects behind Glen Canyon Dam, robbing the river of its abrasive cutting power. The fluting is found only on the surfaces of rock that oppose the force of the river.

34. Mile 55. Above Kwagunt Rapid before sunset.

35. Ripples on a windblown sand bank at the river's edge.

36. Banded gecko.

37. Blue sky and golden canyon walls reflected in the wet sand.

38. Mile 56. Kwagunt Rapid (4–6), reflecting the colors of the sunlit canyon wall beyond.

This is one of the few pictures taken with the camera on a tripod, since a long exposure was necessary.

39. Reflection on the river, photographed with a 200-mm. lens, from a cliff about forty feet above the water.

40. Mile 71. Sunset over the South Rim.

41–44. Canyon specialties: beaver tail cactus; tamarisk, a scorpion; and choya cactus.

45. Mile 71. Backlit ridges near the river at sunrise, across from Cardenas Creek.

46. Mile 93. Dories in the Upper Granite Gorge during an afternoon rain shower.

47. Raven in flight.

48 & 49. Mile 93. Granite Falls at sunset (49) and a pool below (48). A long exposure time produced the soft effect in the water; broken clouds provided the spot lighting on the far wall.

50 & 51. Running Granite Falls (7–8).

52. Mile 95. Hermit Rapid (7–8). Inside the boat, whitewater crashes everywhere.

53. Running Granite Falls in a kayak.

54. Mile 98. Crystal Rapid (7–10). Boatmen run this unusually rocky rapid alone in order to maneuver more easily around the big hole and rocks. This boatman missed a stroke or two at the top of the rapid and hit the corner of the big hole. He lost his right oar at this most critical moment, but made it through the

rest of the rapid without incident.

55. Inside the boat as a wave crashes into the bow. The motorized camera was mounted on a bracket above and behind the boat. A long exposure (1/15th second) was used to capture the feeling of movement. Should the dory tip over, the large orange life jackets will keep the people floating high in the water, until the end of the rapid when the boat is righted.

56. Mile 116½. Elves Chasm. Here, in the shade of the steep, narrow canyon walls, a lush oasis is hidden from the otherwise arid desert environment. A small spring-fed stream flows over the high wall and into the amphitheater below.

57–59. Columbine and maidenhair fern grow in the most shady areas of Elves Chasm. The stream works its way toward the river over falls formed by huge boulders filling the narrow canyon.

60. Mile 134. Cactus and mesquite trees near Tapeats Creek, about one and a half miles up the side canyon from the river.

61. Thunder River, a spring at the base of the Redwall formation that cascades down the face of the sheer cliff to join Tapeats Creek about two miles from its junction with the river.

62. Cottonwood tree and 4 o'clock bush near Tapeats Creek.

63. The clear water of Tapeats Creek (on the left) joins the muddy river (on the right).

An afternoon storm builds as the sun begins to set.

64. On its way to meet the river, Tapeats Creek has undercut the sandstone wall.

65. The canyon wall near Mile 135.

66. Bighorn sheep.

67. Mile 136. Deer Creek Falls (125 feet high), a short walk from the river.

68. Detail of impurities in a limestone boulder makes an interesting abstract pattern. Photographed with a micro lens, this section of the rock is about eight inches across.

69. Scarlet monkey flower.

70. Deer Creek, another of the many spring-fed tributaries of the Colorado, flows inside a narrow gorge in the Tapeats sandstone before reaching the edge of the falls.

71. A redbud tree in the gorge above Deer Creek Falls.

72. Globe mallow.

73–75. Mile 148. Matkatamiba Canyon, carved into the Muav limestone formation, near its confluence with the river. Two hundred yards farther up, the gorge widens and flattens, opening into an amphitheater, through which a small stream runs.

76 & 77. Mile 157. Havasu Creek and Mooney Falls (about two hundred feet high). Calcium carbonate and other chemicals in the water form travertine ledges and pools, and also give the creek its bright blue color. The Havasupai Indians live twelve miles from the river, at the bottom of Havasu Canyon.

78. Mile 160. Muav limestone walls, which form the banks of the river, evoke old Egyptian ruins.

79. Black-necked stilts in flight.

80. Spotted sandpiper.

81. Mile 179. Lava Falls at dawn.

82–87. Dories running Lava Falls (8–10), the ultimate challenge to boatmen on the Colorado. The river here drops thirty-seven feet in about three hundred yards and has been clocked at up to thirty miles per hour. At one time or another, Lava Falls has flipped every type of boat that has attempted to run it, including the motor-driven pontoon rafts.

88 & 91. Mile 180. Columnar basalt remnants of one of the many lava flows that poured into the Canyon about a million years ago, damming the river and creating a lake almost 180 miles long. The river was able to cut its way through the lava dam and return to its original channel, as it will inevitably do to the less durable man-made structures that now block its path.

89. Datura.

90. Lava boulders and sandstone pebbles lie partially buried in the sand.

92–94. Mile 202. Ocotillo and Grand Canyon rattlesnake.

95. Mile 232. Sculptured and polished by the river, the two-billion-year-old schist formation strongly resembles the work of modern artists.

96. Mile 240. In the Lower Granite Gorge below Separation Canyon, where three of Major Powell's men decided their chances of survival would be better if they hiked out of the Canyon rather than face the unknown river ahead. The men were never seen or heard from again. As it turned out, the rest of the Powell party made it to the Grand Wash Cliffs at the end of the Grand Canyon with no mishaps. Separation Rapid and all the others below are now buried by Lake Mead, which backs up forty miles into the Canyon behind Hoover Dam.

97. Polished schist in the Lower Granite Gorge.

98. Snowy egrets in flight.

99. At the end of the day.

A Word on the Photography

The photographs in this book were taken with 35-mm. single-lens reflex equipment, using Kodachrome film—KII, K25, or K64. While working away from the boat, I carry one camera body and the following lenses: 20, 24, 35, 55 micro, 105, and 200 mm. I use a motor-drive camera when photographing the rapids from either the shore or inside the boat. The only filter I used was a neutral density for one or two of the moving water shots when I wanted a long exposure and couldn't stop the lens down far enough. For those pictures, a tripod was employed to steady the camera.

Camera equipment is stored in water-proof Army surplus ammunition cans, lined with foam. To photograph the rapids from inside the boat, I place the motor-drive camera in an ammo can, with large holes cut out of two opposite sides. Both holes are covered with Plexiglas, and sealed with silicone rubber. One affords the front of the lens a clear view and the other allows me to see through the viewfinder in order to assure proper framing when I attach the rig to the boat. Using an assortment of brackets and clamps, I am able to mount the camera in several different positions. All the settings and adjustments on the camera must be made before the box is sealed at the approach to each rapid. A thin, clear wire runs between the box and a switch that I can trip with my foot. When the boat is in the middle of the roughest water, I start the camera, which will automatically expose an entire roll of film—thirty-six pictures—within nine to eighteen seconds, depending on how I set it. Though the rig is securely mounted on the boat, I frequently attach a spare life jacket to the camera box just in case the boat tips over and the mounting doesn't hold. Fortunately, I've stayed upright for all the rapids in which I used the rig, though I've often wondered just what a flip from inside the boat would look like on film.

Acknowledgments

Although I have never had any formal training in photography, there are four people who have strongly influenced my way of seeing: Dave Bohn, Charles and Ray Eames, and Ernst Haas. I am most grateful to them.

It's a privilege to be associated with Grand Canyon Dories and its crew members, with whom I've had the pleasure of sharing the dories, the river, and the Canyon. I thank them all for their cooperation.

My special thanks go to Jan Malinowski, whose discerning eye was a tremendous help in picking the "top selects" from each summer's shooting.

Finally, I am grateful to the staff of Studio Books at The Viking Press for their assistance in turning a collection of photographs into a book, and for making their office a friendly home away from home. I especially appreciate the efforts of Olga Zaferatos, my editor, and Christopher Holme, the designer.

J.B.